The Planet's
Most Spiritual
Places

The Planet's
Most Spiritual
Places

Malcolm Croft

IVY PRESS

CONTENTS

Chapter 1
Ancient Monuments

Chapter 2
Places of Worship

Chapter 3
Pilgrimages

Chapter 4
Natural Wonders

Chapter 5
Centres of Enlightenment

Chapter 6
Living Landmarks

INTRODUCTION

**"We are not human beings having a spiritual experience.
We are spiritual beings having a human experience."**

Pierre Teilhard de Chardin, French priest, scientist and philosopher.

Welcome to the planet's most spiritual places. Over the course of this journey, we will together trot the globe in search of that elusive quality, spirituality. It has long been humankind's quest to understand its purpose and place in the universe, and this promises to be a first-class flight for the mind, body and soul. Along the way, we will have our breath taken away by a bounty of beautiful destinations, great and small, far and wide, from the mighty peaks of Nepal to the submarine canyon of Nazaré, and plenty more in between.

By the end of this adventure, we'll hopefully have found the various meanings – yes, plural – of life as seen through the eyes and lives of these landmarks, as well as the patrons and pilgrims who worship them from near and afar.

However, in advance of embarking on this spiritual journey towards the Great Before and the Great Beyond, we must first define what spirituality is, and how we've applied this in making our final selection of places. It wasn't easy. Spirituality comes in multiple shapes and sizes, many forms and functions, and can have all sorts of differing significance to citizens from all corners of the world: It is as rare as it is ever-present.

For some, spirituality is something tangible – a touch of a temple wall or a view of a stained-glass window, for example. For others, it is simply something you must feel in your soul.

History teaches us that spirituality is a connection to deities, God and the divine, transmitted through various forms: An embrace of our mind, body and spirit at sunrise or sunset; a baptism of water from a large wave or sacred lake; a pilgrimage to the promised land; His (or Her) presence at a monolithic rock standing solo in a desert: none can be denied.

Spirituality is the metaphysical and physical attachment to that divine ideal that humankind has together placed upon itself over the millennia. It is a sense, a feeling, created in order to gain a better, deeper and more enduring understanding of our world, and how we came to be. In effect, it is to know the unknown. A spiritual moment can be encountered within at any time, wherever you are or whoever you are with. In the same way that meeting a person for the first – or final – time can feel sacred.

Spirituality, simply, is a connection. A connection to this world, to the divine, to each other, to the past, and as the destinations in this book will attest, the physical and symbolic manifestation of Heaven on earth. We have included 100 of those special, sacred, extraordinary landmarks that made a connection, at once grounding us to our world and offering something beyond it.

To define what spirituality is has been the quintessential adventure by every human, tribe or race since their own respective dawns. The search for spirituality, and the places that represent it, binds us together by allowing us to see the world, and their history, through their eyes. As you adventure through this book, you'll soon come to discover that no matter how different each destination may seem, all of them are connected in some way.

Today's world is a super-busy place. Full of noise and stuffed with distraction, each new day bringing more opportunity to gain distance from the spiritual connections that bond us together. We created this book as a moment to pause, reflect – stop – and think about the places of spirituality that exist in front of your eyes, as well as being the ideal travelling companion for explorers seeking inspiration on their next soul-searching spiritual voyage into the unknown, without having to leave home.

We hope you find what you're looking for within...
See you at the next stop.

TIMELINE

The places in this book range in age from millions of years old to only a few decades. In order to give some perspective as to what was happening around the world and when certain monuments were created, these pages show the approximate relative creation or foundation dates of certain places.

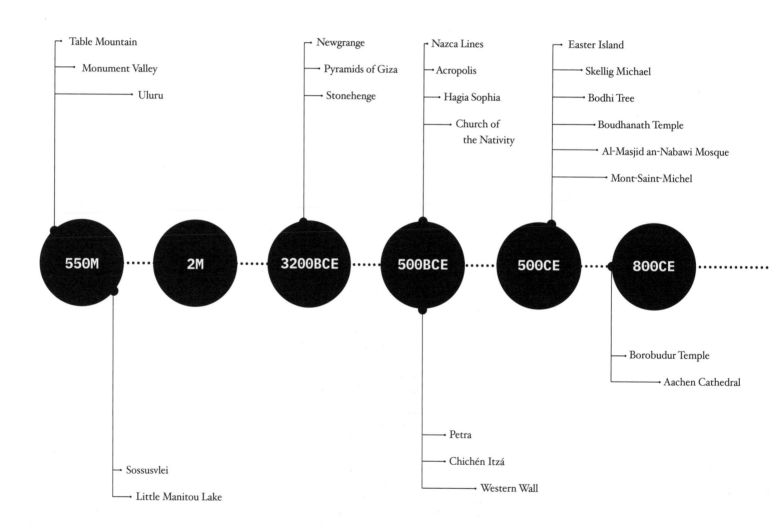

Table Mountain
Monument Valley
Uluru

Newgrange
Pyramids of Giza
Stonehenge

Nazca Lines
Acropolis
Hagia Sophia
Church of the Nativity

Easter Island
Skellig Michael
Bodhi Tree
Boudhanath Temple
Al-Masjid an-Nabawi Mosque
Mont-Saint-Michel

550M   2M   3200BCE   500BCE   500CE   800CE

Sossusvlei
Little Manitou Lake

Petra
Chichén Itzá
Western Wall

Borobudur Temple
Aachen Cathedral

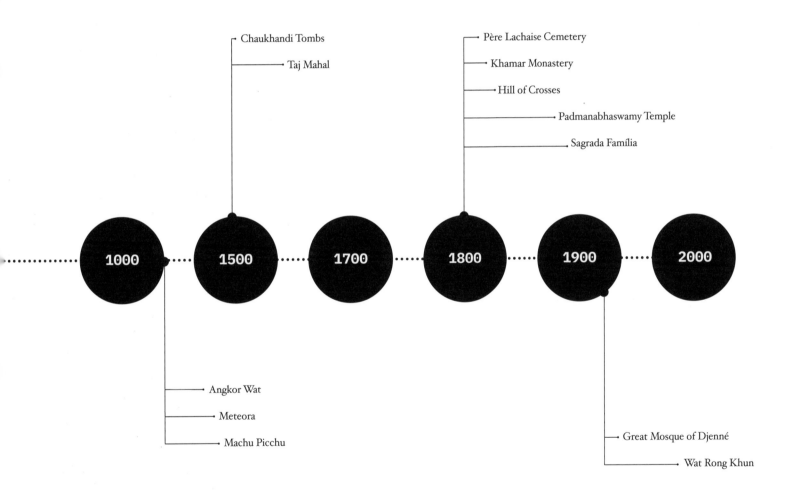

Chaukhandi Tombs

Taj Mahal

Père Lachaise Cemetery

Khamar Monastery

Hill of Crosses

Padmanabhaswamy Temple

Sagrada Família

| 1000 | 1500 | 1700 | 1800 | 1900 | 2000 |

Angkor Wat

Meteora

Machu Picchu

Great Mosque of Djenné

Wat Rong Khun

KEY

⊛ Location

✝ Religion or type

🏛 Origin date of spiritual interest (approximate)

👥 Annual visitors

📅 Best time to visit

📍 Size/height

CHAPTER 1

Ancient Monuments

Humans have pondered the reasons for existence for thousands of years, and have felt the need to worship a form of higher being for almost as long. This has been evidenced all over the world, as monuments were constructed around thanksgiving, homage or devotion in some of the earliest forms of idolization.

Acropolis of Athens

AN ICON OF ANTIQUITY AND THE BIRTHPLACE OF CIVILIZATION

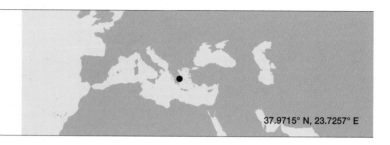

- ✳ Greece
- ✝ Classical
- 🏛 432 BCE
- 👥 2 million
- 📅 October–April
- 🗺 3 hectares (7.4 acres)

37.9715° N, 23.7257° E

Since its foundation in the 5th century BCE, the Acropolis in Athens has been a physical powerhouse that defined humankind's quest for civilization and democracy. And that's not to even discuss its status as an awe-inspiring engineering and architectural masterpiece.

However, perhaps the greatest reason as to why the Acropolis complex has meant so much to so many for so long – and the reason for its spiritual significance today – is because the greatest thinkers of the classical world (Socrates, Plato and Aristotle), all paced this rocky outcrop during its construction ... and contemplated the rules for life. It was here that our fundamental ideas of mathematics, biology, astronomy, atomic theory, democracy, trial by jury, constitutional government, free speech and individual rights were devised, discussed and debated for the very first time. It is no wonder the place has a sense of the supernatural about it. If the pillars of the Parthenon could talk, they would have much to say.

Located on a 3-hectare (7.4-acre) limestone plateau that climbs 150 metres (490 ft) above sea level to overlook the city of Athens, Acropolis Hill, or the Sacred Rock as it is known, remains a spectacular marvel, seemingly impossible then, breathtaking now. The foundation stone of the Acropolis was laid in 460 BCE, when Pericles, a Greek politician and general, commanded Athens into its "Golden Age" by building (and rebuilding) monuments and temples designed to represent the best of humankind.

Within the Acropolis complex are the Erechtheion, the Theatre of Dionysus Eleuthereus and the Temple of Athena Nike. At its heart, however, is the Parthenon. Built to last in order to honour Athena, the goddess of wisdom and war, for eternity. Amazingly, the Parthenon was built in just nine short years, and was completed in 432 BCE. In the time since, it has been a Pagan temple, a Byzantine cathedral, a Christian church and a Muslim mosque, with its religious identity revised regularly.

One of the most outstanding features of the Acropolis is the fact that it still exists. It has survived war, earthquakes, looting, erosion and the impact of tourism – the Acropolis is one of the most popular historical attractions in the world, with more than two million annual visitors.

Greek myths and legends abound where the Acropolis is concerned, but one relating directly to the rock concerns both Poseidon and Athena. The two were competing in order to become named as the patron of the city by the populous. Each god was bestowing gifts and when it was the turn of Poseidon, he tapped the rock of the Acropolis with his famous trident. On the spot he hit, a superb horse came forth, and it was on this very spot that the Erechtheion was erected a number of years later. As any visitor will know, the city was named after Athena, whose gift was an olive tree. Visible from miles around, the Acropolis looks down on the city, as the gods once did from Mount Olympus, making Athens a stunning city to visit.

Opposite: The Parthenon and other buildings within the Acropolis are famed for their gleaming white marble. However, recent laser cleaning of the Parthenon's marble showed it was once painted blue, red and green.

Aksum

THE TALLEST REMAINS OF A VAST KINGDOM FROM THE ANCIENT WORLD

✴ Ethiopia

✝ Ethiopian Orthodox

🏛 400 CE

👥 50,000

📅 October–June

📍 21 metres (69 ft) (height)

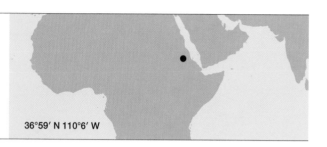

36°59′ N 110°6′ W

The Northern Stelae Park in Ethiopia is a curious place, an open field with some tall towers. But it serves as a reminder of the great civilization that once dominated this corner of the world: the Kingdom of Aksum. These heavy granite towers symbolize an epic story of civilization, colonization and, eventually, destruction.

The Aksumite Empire was a significant one in the Middle Ages, and spanned much of northern Ethiopia, as well as parts of what we today know as Eritrea, Djibouti and Sudan. Evidence of the Aksumite civilization is regularly unearthed throughout that entire area in the shape of coins, ceramics, carvings and more to this day. One of the world's main powers then, alongside China, Persia and Rome, Aksum is now the least known, and historians and travellers must dig deep for evidence, although there is plenty to be found if you know where to look...

The kingdom itself was founded sometime around the beginning of the first millennium starting between BCE and CE, with its conversion to Christianity arriving, officially at least, some 300 or so years after that. With different religions come differing burial rites and ways to remember ancestors. And that is how we arrive in the Northern Stelae Park in Aksum (also called Axum), the city that was the capital of the empire, and an important naval and trading base from around 400 BCE to the 10th century. The park is, effectively, an ancient graveyard of rulers of the empire. But instead of simple gravestones, huge carved edifices were erected in memory of fallen leaders. There are more than 300 of these stelae, but the vast majority have fallen to the ground. Each one is from a single block of granite, and these objects represent some of the largest – and heaviest – man-made monoliths ever to be put up by humankind. One of

the most famous, the Great Stele, is more than 33 metres (108 ft) long and weighs a stunning 520 tonnes (511 tons). Records do not exist of when this huge stone was erected, and it is suspected that it fell over not long after it was put in place – even possibly during installation.

It is without doubt that these structures were built to serve as monuments, and the ground beneath them may contain the tombs of the people they memorialize. Archaeologists believe that the altars that are found at the base of some of the larger stone towers were built with grooves in them, most likely as a runoff outlet for blood during the live sacrifice of a creature. Fortunately, it was most likely for animals rather than humans.

In the surrounding area you will also find what is called the Queen of Sheba's Palace, in Dongur, (also known as the Palace of Makea, as she was known in Ethiopia). This is not an independently or officially verified claim, as the true story of the queen is unknown and much disputed. However, the structure itself was certainly occupied by someone of great importance.

Opposite: The Obelisk of Aksum was only restored to Ethiopia from Italy in 2005. It had been looted from its homeland during Italy's invasion in 1937 and stood in the Piazza di Porta Capenamin in Rome for more than 60 years before its return.

Angkor Wat

A SPRAWLING CITY OF SHRINES AND TEMPLES

✵ Cambodia

✝ Buddhist

🏛 1200

👥 2.6 million

🗓 November–March

📍 1.6 km² (1 sq. mi.)

13°24'45" N 103°52'0" E

Angkor Wat is not just a temple, it's a city. A vast complex of more than 1,000 shrines and monuments, it is the largest spiritual structure in the world by far, and a feast for all the senses.

Located in northwest Cambodia and spread across 160 hectares (395 acres), a similar size to Los Angeles, the first Angkor Wat temple was built by King Suryavarman II, ruler of the Khmer Empire from 1113–1150. It was constructed over the course of four decades as a Hindu temple celebrating the supreme gods Vishnu, Shiva and Brahma. At the time, the temple became famed for its symbolism, symmetry and spirituality and was a source of pride and strength to the Khmer civilization. Even today, the temple is the main symbol of Cambodia and even features on the nation's flag.

After Suryavarman's tenure, the temple was reimagined by King Jayavarman VII as an earthly representation of Mount Meru, the centre of the universe in Buddhist cosmology – a golden mountain, where all the world's oceans meet. He believed that the Hindu gods had failed him, following conquest by modern-day Vietnam. Visitors must cross the 188-metre (617-ft) bridge over one of the largest moats on earth in order to enter the temple complex.

The centrepiece of this amazing city is Angkor Wat Temple, constructed in its stunning quincunx shape: four large towers surround a larger main tower, similar to the positioning of the five dots on a die face. Each tower represents the five peaks of Mount Meru (and the five then-known continents on earth), and is shaped distinctively like a lotus flower, a deeply significant shape in Buddhism and a sacred symbol representing purity, rebirth and strength. The towers were built at precise angles relative to the rising sun on the summer solstice. The largest, the central tower – 65 metres (312 ft) tall – aligns perfectly with the sun's path on the spring equinox. The temple is built of more than 10 million 1.5-tonne (1.4-ton) sandstone blocks, more than all the pyramids in Giza combined. The stone was transported from more than 40 kilometres (25 miles) away, and was brought to the site on boats through man-made canals, which were then converted to create the moat.

The Angkor complex comprises more than 1,000 smaller temples and monuments within its walls, several of which, such as the monastery of Ta Prohm, have been consumed – strangled – by the tree roots of banyan trees, adding an additional supernatural element to the already divine landscape. Today, Angkor is the spiritual home for 80 per cent of Cambodia's Buddhist population – more than 15 million people – making the site the most important pilgrimage site for Buddhists in the world. In 1992, the Angkor complex was designated a World Heritage site by UNESCO, and it is often voted one of the earth's most important places for spiritual retreat and enlightenment.

Opposite: Angkor Wat's main temple (top) was also designed as a funeral site for King Suryavarman. The structure faces west, unlike most other temples at Angkor, suggesting afterlife, and it basks in the embers of a beautiful sunset.

Bagan

STUNNING SUNSETS AND A SEA OF TEMPLES

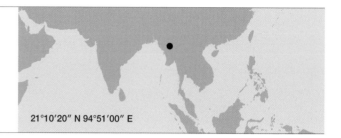

⊛ Myanmar

✝ Theravada Buddhist

🏛 1100

👥 400,000

📅 November–May

🗺 104 km² (40 sq. mi.)

21°10'20" N 94°51'00" E

In recent years, Myanmar has been in the headlines for many reasons, often distracting the outside world from the fact that this Buddhist nation is littered with a sea of spiritual secrets, many of which are yet to be uncovered by the world at large.

Along a bendy banks of the sacred Irrawaddy River stand tall more than 3,500 breathtaking pagodas, stupas, monasteries and religious ruins, described as the "Sea of Temples". This is the most dense concentration of monuments dedicated to Buddha in the entire world. Welcome to Bagan or Arimaddanapura, as it was known 1,000 years ago: the city that tramples on enemies.

Each one of these enormous structures is a salutation to Buddha, the spiritual leader of the country's 90 per cent Theravada Buddhists; in its heyday it was used as sacred space for Buddhist spiritual practice. This compound of temples stretches for more than 10,360 hectares (25,600 acres) peeking out among a flat, thick, green canopy of trees, where the earth is scorched yellow by the hot, dry climate.

The majority of the 3,500 temples were built between 1057 and 1287 during a spree of construction by King Anawrahta, the first ruler of the Pagan Kingdom. He had a desire to unite the Burmese kingdom, as well as wanting to show rival kingdoms far and wide the ingenuity of his Pagan empire through the fierceness of their religious devotion. With the awe-inspiring architectural wonder of each individual temple, Bagan soon garnered a deserved reputation as a centre for religion and study, and it also became the kingdom's capital city.

In its infancy, the people of Bagan – Pagans – proudly built more than 10,000 pagodas to Buddha with a height of 40 metres (131 ft), with Thatbyinnyu Temple, the tallest one, reaching more than 61 metres (201 ft) into the sky. Sadly, more than three-quarters of these towers have collapsed over the centuries, mainly because of the size and scale of earthquakes the region receives, and due to its position on a major seismic belt. A particularly serious earthquake in 1975 did the most damage, reducing more temples to rubble than any other earthquake in a 1,000-year period.

Unlike other world temple compounds – such as Chichén Itzá in Mexico or Borobudur in India – the stupas, temples and pagodas in Bagan can be freely climbed upon and explored by tourists and adventurers looking for that perfect photo of the unfolding landscape. Standing atop one of the largest temples – Ananda or Htilominlo Pahto, for example – at sunset and looking out across the sea of buildings, reflecting on their place in the world, has long been sought out by spiritual seekers as a definitive sacred experience and a sight to behold in their minds for the rest of their days. Stunning colour fills the sky at sundown and sunup, only adding to the effect.

In 2019, UNESCO awarded the site World Heritage status, and it remains a hugely popular place of pilgrimage for the 50 million Myanmar Buddhists.

Opposite: Rising from the morning mists, the Mahabodhi Temple – the Great Awakening Temple as it is also known – is an exact replica of the world-famous Bodh Gaya Temple in India (*see* page 206).

Borobudur

A MAN-MADE MANDALA THAT NAVIGATES TO NIRVANA

⊛ Thailand

✝ Buddhist

🏛 760 CE

👥 4 million

📅 April–October

🗺 2.5 km² (1 sq. mi.)

7.608° S 110.204° E

Borobudur is the world's grandest Buddhist temple in terms of size, stature and significance. It is, quite simply, divine in every element of its being. From geometry to geography, geomancy to geology, it is a blessed monument to Buddhism's belonging, and a profound yearning to understand humankind's place in the universe.

Built from more than two million stone blocks, of a bluish-grey volcanic stone known as andesite, Borobudur's colossal construction alone is worthy of the world's interest. But that is just the beginning of its wonder.

It is shaped in the form of a mandala, a geometric configuration of symbols that alludes to a greater meaning. In Borobudur's case, a step pyramid consisting of nine stacked platforms, six square and three circular, topped by a large central dome. Its architectural purpose is to represent a spiritual journey through three ascending spherical realms: Kāmadhātu (desire), the square base Rūpadhātu (form), the five concentric square terraces; and Arūpadhātu (formlessness), the three circular platforms and the central stupa. As with many Buddhist monuments and temples, the mandala at Borobudur takes its shape and form from the mythical Mount Meru, the Buddhist symbol representing the centre of the universe – the square depicts earth and the circle, heaven. Altogether, this architecture transcends its earthly form to become a spiritual centre of divine enlightenment that guides Buddhists towards a higher state of consciousness, a blending of Buddhism's central tenets: ancestor worship and the quest of attaining nirvana. Surrounding the Arūpadhātu level are 72 stupas, each containing a statue of the Buddha. From above, Borobudur is almost unbelievable in sheer size and scope.

Built throughout the 8th and 9th centuries CE, during the reign of the Syailendra dynasty, Borobudur became the region's main pilgrimage and spiritual centre point for Java's Buddhists – as well as for those from further afield – until some time in the 1500s, when it was abandoned. This was possibly due to the arrival of Islam or when the capital of the Medang Kingdom was moved to the region of East Java. Borobudur became lost, and was swiftly reclaimed by nature, almost sinking into the deep jungle that surrounded this incredible, and now remote, site.

Borobudur lay hidden under thick layers of volcanic ash and was overgrown by jungle for more than 300 years, until 1814. It was rediscovered by Hermann Cornelius who was travelling under the orders of Thomas Stamford Raffles, the Lieutenant Governor-General in charge of establishing British rule on Java, following a military campaign against the French. Cornelius and his men spent months burning 2,500 square metres (26,909 sq. ft) of dense vegetation to reveal what lay beneath. What a sight – and a stunning spiritual encounter – that must have been.

Opposite: Located at the centre of Java in the Kedu Valley, between twin volcanoes and two rivers, Borobudur's geography is sacred, and purposefully placed because of its super-fertile volcanic soils. That soil would later reclaim the site.

Chaukhandi

MESMERIZING MAUSOLEUMS IN A SUN-SCORCHED CEMETERY

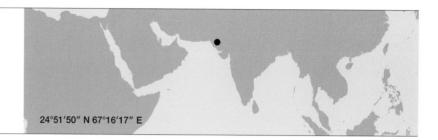

⊛ Pakistan

† Islam

▥ 1500

👥 Unknown

📅 May–October

👣 5 km² (2 sq. mi.)

24°51′50″ N 67°16′17″ E

Forty kilometres (25 miles) east of Pakistan's capital city, Karachi, lies a large Islamic cemetery of the once powerful and prominent. The above-ground graves are as haunting as the site is supposedly haunted.

Translated as "the four corners", Chaukhandi takes its name from the compound of more than 600 well preserved yellow sandstone necropolises – more than 1,500 of them in total lie in ruins – of the holy warriors of Muhammad bin Qasim and the powerful tribal chiefs who ruled this sacred, scorched landscape in the distant past. Bin Qasim was the first Muslim to capture Hindu regions and start the foundations of Muslim rule.

Each of these crypts lies, uniquely, approximately 4 metres (14 ft) above ground and is 2.5 metres (8 ft) long, supported by a hand-carved column on each of four sides. The more influential the chief, the higher from the ground lies the grave. This sacred burial site is Pakistan's most treasured national heritage wonder and is on the list of inscriptions for UNESCO as a site of significant historical interest; it seems sure to be accredited soon.

The geometrically identical mausoleums are, indeed, works of intricate wonder that are believed to have been built and installed over a 300-year period from the 15th century CE. The construction, decoration and burial styles are all unique to the region of Sindh, which is located near the coast in the south of Pakistan – and no other Islamic burial grounds look anything like this one, making it all the more rewarding if a visit to this remarkable place is possible.

Each tomb is rectangular in shape and adorned with exquisitely elaborate carvings, each one telling a different tale – recalling epic stories of the men and women whose relics lie within, as well as symbols signifying their high status, life

and causes of death. The carvings on some of the male graves depict horsemen with shields, swords, bows and arrows. The women's graves include ornaments and jewellery to indicate the wealth of that individual. The huge sandstone tombs and their carvings reveal not just the reverence with which these chieftains and their families were held by the tribe, but also the skill of the architects that stacked the heavy slabs into pyramid shapes. The precise positioning of the tombs is very uncommon and curious, too, with the bodies buried in a south-to-north orientation – not east-to-west like other gravesites, even those that are relatively close by. The reason for this was not recorded and remains unknown, but it could have something to do with a way of highlighting the power and influence of the bodies that lie within.

Pakistan is now home to more than 200 million Muslims – that's more than 95 per cent of the nation's population – and many of them undertake a pilgrimage to Chaukhandi, the site being a short distance from their country's capital. Once in the large graveyard, visitors can freely explore the monuments to Muhammad bin Qasim's warriors and are also able to pray for their sacrifice to the Muslim cause.

Opposite: Chaukhandi has a reputation for being haunted – it is said that the spirits of the dead roam at night. Locals advise tourists not to venture to the gravesite after sundown.

Chichén Itzá

A SPIRITUAL SALUTE TO THE SUN … AND A SERPENT

⊛ **Mexico**

✝ **Mayan**

🏛 **312 BCE**

👥 **2 million**

📅 **Spring** (20 March) **and Autumn Equinox**

📍 **10 km² (4 sq. mi.)**

20°40′58.4″ N 88°34′7.0″ W

Mexico's Yucatan Peninsula is known for being the home of many earth-shattering sites, from the asteroid that caused the demise of the dinosaurs to Chichén Itzá, a stunning city of Mayan ruins with awe-inspiring ancestry.

At the heart of the small city of Chichén Itzá lies its most cherished attraction – El Castillo – the iconic step pyramid and tallest structure in the city, reaching a peak at 30 metres (98 ft) that far exceeds the horizon line. This eye-catching limestone attraction was lifted into the sky more than 1,500 years ago, and its original purpose was a sun salutation and astronomical calendar for the Mayan civilization that roamed and ruled the peninsula for more than 500 years. During their tenure of the land, the Mayans developed an advanced culture that was built on the foundations of architectural, agricultural and engineering genius – skills and techniques that would influence the region for 1,000 years, long after their disappearance. Chichén Itzá is unarguably the zenith of this excellence.

As structurally sound as El Castillo is, it is the spiritual features that are of key importance. The pyramid is a temple in honour of the feathered serpent deity Kukulcán, the creator god, and the god of life, rain, wind and storms, the representation of the divine on earth in Mayan culture. It is a precursor to the Aztec serpent-bird god, Quetzalcoatl, established a millennia after Kukulcán. Feathered serpents have a long history of being deities throughout ancient Mesoamerica: they were able to live below and above the earth, a symbol for the uniting of the gods above with humanity below.

El Castillo is a masterpiece of astronomical proportions, too. Each of its four sides has 91 steps, with a final top step added to make a total of 365 steps – one for each day of the year. The Mayans constructed the pyramid so that it marks the summer and autumn equinoxes – the two days of the year when there are equal amounts of day and night (winter and summer solstices celebrate the shortest/longest day of the year). Magically, at sunset on these equinoxes, the sun's descent creates a shadow that represents the appearance of a serpent slithering down the steps. It is a truly supernatural experience, should you be lucky enough to witness it.

Other wonders that are located around the Chichén Itzá area include the Great Ball Court (incidentally the largest playing field in Mesoamerica), the Temple of the Warriors (featuring ancient imagery of human-heart-eating), and the Sacred Cenote – the spirit-infused, water-filled sinkhole with mystical healing properties. It is this sinkhole that gives the nearby compound its name: *Chichén Itzá* means "the mouth at the well of Itza", with Itza translated as "water magicians" and derived from the Mayan *Itz* for "magic" and *á* for "water".

The entire area makes for a supremely magical, mystical, mysterious experience, indeed.

Opposite: Visitors are invited to clap their hands in front of the El Castillo pyramid. Those who do should hear a simultaneous echo that simulates the serpent's rattle and a bird's chirp.

Ciudad Perdida

A JUNGLE CITY THAT WAS LOST FOR 1,000 YEARS

- ✴ Colombia
- ✝ N/A
- 🏛 800 CE
- 👥 20,000
- 📅 December–March
- 📍 1.2 hectares (2.9 acres)

11°2'16.79" N 73°55'30.69" W

Accessible only by a 42-kilometre (26-mile)-trek through the jungle, the Ciudad Perdida, or "lost city" is a haven of peace and quiet. Many mysteries surround this once-teeming city, but popularity is increasing, and with tourists come troubles…

As you would imagine from a lost city, not a great deal is known for sure about its origins or the people who once lived in it. What we do know, however, is that deep in the Colombian jungle, around 800 CE, lived a people known as the Tayrona. They inhabited a number of small villages in the Sierra Nevada de Santa Marta mountains, a coastal range located in the far north of Colombia. The mountain range is notable for being the highest coastal range in the world, its tallest peak reaching 5,700 metres (18,700 ft) above sea level. It is inhospitable terrain for a variety of reasons, but tribes did settle, and what we today call Cuidad Perdida was most likely an administrative and trading centre for people from surrounding villages.

Evidence of habitation from around 800 CE shows that the city was populated some 650 years before Machu Picchu (*see* page 36), the Peruvian mountain city in the sky.

As with many other sites in South and Central America, seismic changes occurred following the arrival of the Spanish in the 15th century and the hundreds of years afterwards. The inhabitants of the lost city disappeared, abandoning their living and trading quarters and leaving no written history. A number of artefacts were left, dating the exodus to some time in the late 15th or early to middle 16th centuries. It is thought that the native dwellers left for more remote quarters, as far as possible from the marauding hordes and the destruction that they bought with them in their quest for gold. Being so remote, and surrounded by such dense jungle, the city was swallowed up. Once-busy tiled roads, carefully constructed terraces (more than 160 of them) and open plazas were lost from view; repossessed by the jungle.

The local descendants of the Tayrona, the Arhuaco, Koguis and Wiwas people reputedly knew about the ruins but kept quiet, preferring to let the plants take over.

This remained the case until 1972, when a group of hunters came across some remains, specifically one of the long stone staircases that lead upwards to more plazas. It is said that the city was looted multiple times, with various ceramic and gold artefacts turning up for sale in local cities. This came to the attention of various official bodies, and archaeologists gained access to the site and carried out much work, up until 1982.

To visit the lost city today requires dedication and personal fitness, for the long trek through the sweltering heat of the steaming jungle is no stroll. And even on arrival the trial continues, with access to the city involving the ascent of a 1,200-step stone staircase that winds up through the clouds. But the rewards are great, and it is unlike any other city you will ever visit, populated or abandoned.

Opposite: The number of visitors to the city has increased steadily since a tourist route was firmly established, early in the 21st century. More vendors and accommodations are planned.

Delphi

A SACRED SANCTUARY AT THE CENTRE OF THE WORLD

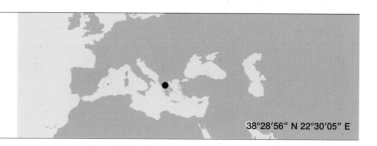

✦ Greece

✝ Classical

🏛 800 BCE

👥 500,000

📅 March–May

⚲ 50 hectares (123 acres)

38°28′56″ N 22°30′05″ E

After almost 3,000 years, the ruins of Delphi still remain an unparalleled sacred site of antiquity. If you're looking for the centre of the world, look no further…

When it comes to timeless spirituality, the Ancient Greeks are unmatched. On the top of a sun-drenched escarpment on Mount Parnassus, 500 metres (1,640 ft) above the valley floor is where Delphi is located, shining as the spotlight of spirituality for the classical world.

Dedicated to the mythological deity Apollo – god of light, knowledge and harmony – Delphi was revered for more than 1,000 years as the religious centre and the symbol of unity of the Ancient Greek world. For centuries, kings, leaders, seats of power, city-states and important historical figures would send priceless gifts to Delphi in the hope of currying favour with the gods.

Also known as the "Delphic Panhellenic Sanctuary", Delphi was considered by the Ancient Greeks as the precise centre of the world. According to myth, the mighty Zeus – god of thunder and sky, and king of the gods – in his quest to find the world's centre point, released two eagles. One bird flew east, the other west. After they had simultaneously flown around the world at equal speed, the point at which they met again was in Delphi. Zeus marked the place with a stone monument known as the omphalos, and that spot became famed as the "earth's navel", a position unchanged for centuries.

Today, the ruins of Delphi are an important global archaeological site, recognized by UNESCO in 1987 for outstanding universal value. As UNESCO stated, "The layout of Delphi is a veritable masterpiece, a series of monuments whose modular elements – terraces, temples, treasuries, etc. combine to form a strong expression of the physical and moral values of a site which may be described as magical." This brings many visitors every year.

The most famous of these structures, perhaps, is Tholos, a medieval circular stone structure, the Delphi Theatre and the Temple of Apollo. Also much visited are the gymnasium, stadium and the Castalian spring. The latter being the once-sacred location where pilgrims to Delphi would quench their thirst before consulting the Oracle, the high priestess Pythia. She, as legend tells, would predict the future for the Athenian senate that would congregate at Delphi's monuments and treasures. Famed throughout history by many other countries and cultures, there is even a famous Eugène Delcaroix painting named *Lycurgus Consulting the Pythia*. An imaginative piece, it shows the high priestess elevated above the man, who has sacrificed a lamb before her. Unfortunately, there exist almost no details of how Pythia actually undertook her duties – contemporary accounts thought it so obvious they didn't bother to record them.

Walking through the warm, balmy mountainside it is not hard to imagine finding answers to many questions here.

Opposite: From 591 BCE, and every eight years, Delphi hosted the Pythian Games at the Hippodrome, to honour Greek deities. The main event was a musical competition.

Easter Island

MYSTERIOUS MONOLITHS AND MYTHS OF ANCIENT WORSHIP

⊛ Chile

✝ Native

🏛 300 CE

👥 100,000

📅 April–June; October/December

🗺 163 km² (63 sq. mi.)

27°7′ S 109°22′ W

Standing guard on an island considered to be the world's most remote destination, the monolithic *moai* (statues) of Chile's Easter Island tell a story submerged in a timeless spirituality.

If you're looking to get away from the stresses of modern life and are seeking a secluded sanctuary to recharge your spiritual energies, Easter Island will not disappoint. And there is nowhere in the world further away from it all – literally. The next nearest land on which to stand is Pitcairn Island – 2,075 kilometres (1,289 miles) away. Mainland Chile, the nation this island belongs to, is more than 3,700 kilometres (2,299 miles) of Pacific Ocean away. But don't worry, if you come to visit, you'll never be alone...

Dotted seemingly randomly around the perimeter of this majestic and mysterious island of 163 square kilometres (63 square miles) are 900 colossal carved stone heads. The average statue is around 4.4 metres (14 ft 6 in.) tall and weighs over 14 tonnes (14 tons). The heads are spread out half a mile from each other, standing atop stone platforms, known as *ahu*.

These magnificent monolithic sculptures are believed to represent the powerful rulers of the island's first ten Polynesian tribes – the Rapa Nui – and their ancestors who first settled here more than 1,800 years ago, sometime after 300 CE. The first Polynesian chief adventurer to the island, and settler, was Hotu Matu'a. He is known as the supreme chief. It is believed the tribe chiefs were imbued with a great power and spiritual knowledge beyond mortals, the magical "mana". When a chief passed on, their body was interred beneath the *ahu*, with a large stone placed upright above it, facing inland, before carving took place. The eyes of the moai were lined with coral for the whites of the eyes and obsidian for the corneas. The Rapa Nui believed they had to

retain the magical power of the chiefs and transmit their "mana" back into the island in order to be protected. Legend tells of how Hotu Matu'a's royal advisor and prophet, Hau-Maka, had a dream voyage in which his spirit was possessed by the Polynesian god Make-Make, who told him to travel to a faraway land for King Hotu Matu'a to rule. It predicted the imminent collapse of the Rapa Nui homeland, the Hiva, which is suspected to have been the Marquesas Islands in French Polynesia.

On top of this mysticism, Easter Island – so named by the first recorded European visitor, the Dutch explorer Jacob Roggeveen, who hit shore on Easter Sunday, 5 April 1722 – is not technically an island. It's a volcano. And one that emerges more than 3,048 metres (10,000 ft) above the Pacific Ocean floor. The oldest known name of the island is *Te Pito o Te Henua*, meaning "the navel of the world" – locals believed it was the centre of the earth.

A fascinating, unique place to visit, Easter Island is not somewhere you can easily end up by accident. Flights from Chile arrive and depart daily, and although this is an established tourist destination, if you time your visit well, it can feel like you have managed to escape to a real lost island paradise. With 900 friendly human heads for company.

Opposite: Easter Island was awarded UNESCO World Heritage status in 1995 for the amazing array of statues. Visitors come from far and wide to witness first-hand the wonderful carvings.

Luxor Temple

CORONATIONS FOR KINGS IN THE CITY OF PALACES

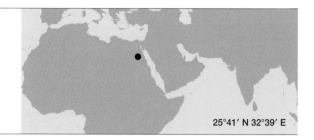

- ☀ Egypt
- ✝ Ancient Egyptian
- ☷ 1400 BCE
- ⛊ 14 million
- ⛾ March–April; October–November.
- ⛾ 417 km² (161 sq. mi.)

25°41' N 32°39' E

For 3,000 years, Luxor Temple has been the resting place for many powerful pharaohs and antiques of Ancient Egypt. Its majesty is matched only by the memories its walls must contain. Thankfully, these walls can talk...

The hundreds of millions of treasure hunters who have visited the city of Luxor in its long-standing history as one of the world's most popular pilgrimage places of antiquity know just how spiritually spectacular it is. It feels at the same time of this world, yet entirely of another.

Luxor, a city covering an enormous surface area along the east bank of the Nile, sits on the ruins of the ancient citadel of Thebes, the pharaohs' seat of power at the height of their rule, a reign that ran for 1,600 years. The city contains two colossal ancient monuments that define the architectural superpower that was Ancient Egypt: Luxor Temple and Karnak Temple, which is 1.6 kilometres (1 mile) north. These two temples were once connected to each other via a 3-kilometre (two-mile)-long road that was lined with over 1,300 human-headed stone sphinxes and known as the Avenue of Sphinxes.

Before Luxor Temple became a burial site hosting the relics of beloved Egyptian kings such as Amenhotep and Ramses II, it was the ancient world's pre-eminent coronation site, the place where kings became pharaohs. This includes the mighty and hugely famous Tutankhamun, whose royal tomb was found across the river, in the Valley of the Kings. This vast compound of temples, tombs, statues, monuments and Ancient Egyptian relics is known as Ipet Resyt – the southern sanctuary.

Construction began on this huge temple in 1400 BCE under the order of Amenhotep III, and was continued by Tutankhamun

(1336–1327 BCE), then Horemheb (1323–1295 BCE) and completed by Ramses II (1279–1213 BCE). It is considered the very height of Egyptian civilization and architectural genius. Built from Nubian sandstone, Luxor Temple isn't dedicated to a specific god or pharaoh like other nearby temples. Instead, it is a celebration of the "rejuvenation of kingship", the reincarnation process whereby the supreme deity, Amun, the god of air – and one of the eight primordial Egyptian deities – was rebirthed with each new coronation of a pharaoh.

Luxor Temple became a spiritual home for the Romans, who adapted the buildings for use as their own religious purposes, and in medieval times Christians and Muslims alike used the chapels as churches and mosques. Luxor Temple, therefore, has been a base for a wide variety spiritual beliefs, each occupier recognizing the sacred power of the stones. Today, the iconic temple and its surrounding compound are famously regarded as the "world's greatest open-air museum", a place where the old world becomes one with the new, as it was with the worship of Amun thousands of years ago. It was one of the first places to be inscribed as a UNESCO World Heritage Site, in 1979.

Opposite: The main visitor hotspots of the Luxor temple complex are the Temple of Seti I, at Gurnah, the Temple of Hatshepsut, at Deir el Bahri, and the Temple of Ramses II.

Machu Picchu

THE LOST CITY OF THE INCAS

⊛ Peru

✝ Inca

🏛 1420

👥 1.5 million

📅 November–May

⊛ 326 km² (126 sq. mi.)

13°09′48″ S 72°32′44″ W

Once this citadel in the clouds was unveiled to the outside world, it instantly became not just the most iconic symbol of the once-buried Inca civilization, but also a sign that the ancient world's spirit still possesses the power to surprise.

Machu Picchu is, simply, one of the most mesmerizing man-made monuments ever constructed. Just to reach its postcard-perfect peak, visitors must first climb more than 100 separate flights of stone staircases, each one individually carved out of a huge slab from stone bought from below. Once at the top – 2,430 metres (7,970 ft) above sea level – an impressive fortress unfolds before your eyes in a most spectacular and dramatic setting. Embedded into a steep ridge and surrounded by a tropical mountain forest, precisely where the Peruvian Andes mountains and the Amazon Basin merge (in the old Quechua language, *Machu Picchu* means "Old Mountain"), Machu Picchu's 200 astronomical, agricultural, ceremonial and religious stone structures – from baths to buildings and from temples to tombs – come together to form something truly out of this world.

Often referred to as the Lost City of the Incas, Machu Picchu demonstrates the pinnacle of the Incas' architectural achievements, and as an astronomical observatory it boasts just how intelligent and in touch with the stars the Incas were (a skill borrowed from the Mayans and Olmecs, and gifted to the Aztecs). The sacred Intihuatana stone accurately highlights the spring and autumn equinoxes, when the sun lands directly over the stone and casts no shadow.

The precise purpose of the city remains a mystery, as the Incas – unlike the Mayans – had no written language. However, historians believe the city existed as a royal estate, constructed in honour of one of the original Inca emperors, Pachacuti (1438–1472), as well as a ceremonial centre that included animal sacrifices.

One of the compound's most cryptic features is the crisscrossing terraces, giant walls and ramps made out of substantial slabs of stone. The Incas, considered the best stonemasons around, used stones that weighed more than 22 kg (50 pounds) to build the city. These stones must have been pushed up the steep mountain side manually, because the rock does not originate from the top. The stone temples and buildings inside the city walls were built using a technique called ashlar, where stones are cut so precisely that they fit together without mortar. Take a close look and you'll see that not even a knife blade can slip between the joints – advanced engineering in a time before the word technology even existed.

Most visitors ascend the steep stairs and slopes in the hope of gaining a better understanding of how the Incas once lived. These visits ensure the Incas' light never goes out again, and that their name, heritage and fascinating customs live on in the hearts and minds of the world's population.

Opposite: The conquest of the Spanish from the 15th century destroyed almost all of the Inca treasures, but as Machu Picchu is hidden up high – invisible from below – the structure managed to survive.

Nazca Lines

A WORSHIP OF WATER IN THE DESERT SAND

- ✴ Peru
- ✝ Nazca
- 🏛 500 BCE
- 👤 50,000
- 📅 December–March
- 🗺 750 km² (290 sq. mi.).

14°43′ S 75°08′ W

The Nazca Lines are the world's most famous lines drawn in the sand. But beyond just being impossible images, this collection of continuous line compositions points to a spiritual civilization yearning to impress the gods above.

In terms of extent, magnitude, quantity, size and diversity, the Nazca Lines, as a spiritual connection to a long-forgotten people, are unparalleled anywhere in the world. More than just a "couple" of line drawings best seen from the air, as many casual observers first believe, the Nazca Lines are much more divine. Altogether, there are more than 1,200 drawings spread out over a surface area of a 750 square kilometres (290 sq. miles), 800 of which are super-straight lines that run, impossibly, for more than 48 kilometres (30 miles). There are geometric shapes and patterns, too – around 800 – as well as 70 zoomorphic shapes (including a spider, fish, condor, heron, monkey, hummingbird, lizard, dog, cat and a giant human). Some are as large as 365 metres (1,200 ft) long – the height of the Empire State Building. The combined length of all the lines is over 1,300 kilometres (800 miles), and historians believe there are hundreds of lines yet to be discovered, possibly even more.

Located in the arid Peruvian coastal plain south of the capital Lima, the Nazca drawings were composed by the Nasca people, who first took their lines for a walk more than 2,500 years ago, and kept on drawing for 2,000 years. The lines are an extraordinary example of how they chose to marry the magical and religious worlds that the Nasca worshipped, by transforming the vast desert into a highly symbolic ritual site. But, with limited stones around to make temples, the Nasca used the land by attaching rope to a wooden stake and drawing lines in the sand.

Recent research suggests that the purpose of the Nazca Lines was spiritual in nature – not astronomical, as once suspected. The Nasca believed that their gods took the form of condors and flew over the plain, and the lines were a simple act of spiritual devotion intended to impress their gods enough to make them send rain, a valuable commodity in the arid lands of the Peruvian coastal plain. The more intricate the pattern, the more impressed the gods would be.

Somewhat ironically, the Nasca people began to decline 750 CE, due, it is suspected, to the effects of El Niño (the warming of sea surface temperature and water rising that is concentrated in the central-east equatorial Pacific), which triggered widespread and destructive flooding. The huge drawings stayed.

Over the years, scientists, historians and sociologists have gazed in wonder at the fascinating images and much discussion has been had about their true purpose. The lines converge on the horizon at the southern hemisphere's winter solstice, but even this fact does not give us the meaning behind the marks.

Opposite: The Nazca lines are, in fact, what is known as a negative image. Instead of being drawn, the top layer of scorched red sand is pushed aside to reveal a whiter sand rock underneath. Some of the most famous drawings are pictured here, clockwise from top left: The Condor (national symbol of Peru); the Spiral (reputedly a labyrinth); the Monkey; the Giant.

Newgrange

LIGHT AND STONE COMBINE FOR WORSHIP OF CONCEPTION FROM THE STARS

✳ Ireland	👥 200,000
✝ Prehistoric	📅 May–September
🏛 3200 BCE	📍 7.7 km² (3 sq. mi.)

53°41'41" N 6°28'32" W

At around 500 years older than the Great Pyramids of Giza, and predating even ancient Stonehenge in England, Ireland's Newgrange was constructed around 3200 BCE. But its old age is just one of its many interesting elements, as its origin story demonstrates...

Perhaps one of the greatest examples in Western Europe of a stone monument known as a passage tomb, the astronomical placement of Newgrange's Great Stone Circle and ancient tomb, means the site can be regarded as the world's oldest solar observatory – and as a celebration of the miracle act of conception. And, with that, its spirituality comes as standard, with many ancient legends and myths elevating it to be without doubt the Republic of Ireland's most sacred spiritual location.

Located in County Meath, in the Boyne Valley in Ireland's ancient east, Newgrange is surrounded by many other hugely historical ancient sites of cultural and spiritual importance, including the Hill of Tara, Hill of Slane, the Abbey of Kells, Trim Castle and Slane Castle. The landmark itself consists primarily of an 85-metre (279-ft) wide and 12-metre (39-ft) high mound made of alternating layers of earth and stones, with a facade of white quartz stones and a grassy top. All told, it consists of about 200,000 tonnes (196,841 tons) of material and covers 4,500 square metres (1.1 acres) of ground. The mound is believed to have been built by Stone Age farmers, and its purpose was originally to honour not just the winter solstice but one of Ireland's greatest myths.

On the winter solstice, beams of light from the rising sun enter the top (known as the roof-box) of the monument and illuminate an underground passage and the ancient burial chamber. The tomb is filled with light for just 17 magical minutes a year. The interior layout of Newgrange has a further curious characteristic: the entrance, inner passage and burial chamber resemble the female reproductive organs, elevating the ancient spiritual elements even further.

According to ancient Irish mythology, the original purpose for the site was to act as a representation of the birth of Aengus, the forbidden child of Chief Dagda Mór, (ruler of the Tuatha Dé Danann, (a supernatural race in Irish mythology; a tribe of the gods), and his love, Boann, the goddess of the river Boyne. The penetration of light at the winter solstice, during which time the sunbeam (representing Dagda) enters the inner chamber (representing the womb of Boann) and the sun's path stops in the centre of chamber, represents the conception of their child, Aengus. Astronomically, the conception of Aengus represents the rebirth of the sun at the winter solstice.

It is fascinating to think, when visiting the area, that ancient visitors travelled far and wide to time their visits with the winter solstice, for there is no evidence of a large settlement of people close by. Newgrange remains largely mysterious, as do the other significant tombs close by, Knowth and Dowth.

Opposite: Newgrange's construction took three decades, with a workforce of approximately 300 people. Only stone tools were used.

Persepolis

A RUINED CITY AT THE FOOT OF THE MOUNTAINS OF MERCY

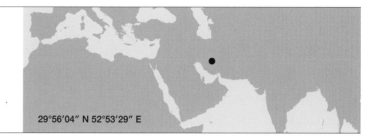

- ✳ Iran
- ✝ Classical
- 🏛 515 CE
- 👤 2 million
- 📅 March–May; Sept–Nov
- 🗺 13 hectares (33 acres)

29°56′04″ N 52°53′29″ E

The almost mythical city of Persepolis was lost for years in the sands of time – as well as the desert. This once-great centre of myth and legend is now a well-preserved archaeological site of huge sociological, historical and spiritual interest to visitors from around the world.

The end of Persepolis, which occurred around 330 BCE, coincided with the end of the empire that built it. Following the destruction of the city by the forces of Alexander the Great of Macedonia that swept through the Middle East, the entire Persian empire crumbled. But what a legacy to have left the world, and now, some 2,500 years later, the site is regarded as possibly the finest and most significant in the entire world.

Inaugurated by the king Darius I (522–486 BCE), and then added to steadily by his son and grandson Xerxes I (486–465 BCE) and Artaxerxes I (465–424 BCE) respectively, the city was intricately planned and carefully constructed using techniques that are still admired to this day. It is, essentially, a large complex of buildings and spaces that were constructed on top of a raised terrace, most of which rose naturally from the desert; the other half was man-made. The quality of architecture and construction meant that some parts of the city are still standing, thousands of years after the city's ruins were abandoned.

But Persepolis was not just a simple city built to house a king, his trusted advisors and the kingdom's administrators. It was designed as a centre of celebration, for people to visit and feast with the king, to be received within the beautiful city walls and to worship the gods there. Although little is known about how the Persians worshipped at that time, the conflict between good and evil was central to it. The most powerful god was

Ahura Mazda, an all-good and all-powerful deity. By the time Persepolis was adorned with carvings, Zoroastrian symbols were well established and commonplace.

It is for the sheer number and quality of carvings that Persepolis is perhaps most famous, and it is for those same carvings that UNESCO added the site to its list of important places of historical significance, calling it "one of the world's greatest archaeological sites, among those which have no equivalent and which bear witness of a unique quality to a most ancient civilization".

This is clearly visible to today's visitors, and the absolute majesty of the columns, gateways and stairs that rise up from the ground is simply astonishing. To have been a visitor at a celebration in the presence of the king would truly have been a magnificent sight. Tourists can walk around the city and gaze in wonder at the craftsmanship that went into the construction of a complex that has lasted for thousands of years. Forgotten by many, the columns have stood the test of time, and are the reason archaeologists were able to locate and then uncover so much of the original place.

Opposite: Although Persepolis was the seat of government for the Achaemenid Empire (also known as the First Persian Empire, 552–330 BCE), it was not the biggest city in the area.

Petra

THE ROSE CITY WITH ITS HISTORY AND LEGACY CARVED INTO ROCK

⊛ Jordan

✝ Classical

🏛 312 BCE

👥 1.1 million

📅 March–May; Sept–Nov

📍 264 km² (102 sq. mi.)

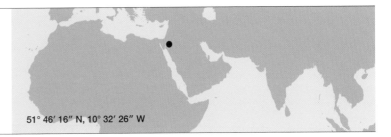

51° 46' 16" N, 10° 32' 26" W

Buried deep in the sands of the Jordanian desert, the once "lost" city of Petra is home to 1,000 royal tombs, each of which is carved into iconic pink-hued sandstone.

Established circa 312 BCE, Petra is one of the oldest, and most archaeologically vital, locations in the world. It is also perhaps the only city on earth where stunning structures are half-carved into rock in such abundance. It is truly unique and incredible, never ceasing to draw gasps of both astonishment and delight from its huge amount of annual visitors.

Surrounded by vast valleys laced with labyrinthine passages and deep-cut gorges – locations once famously walked by Moses in his epic biblical quest – Petra was established by the Nabatean Empire at the turn of the millennium between BCE and CE. The Nabateans were nomadic Arabs who, by settling, kickstarted one of the most advanced prehistoric civilizations in human history. For example, they were one of the first to invent a water management system that allowed the capture of water in a notably thirsty landscape. Petra was also a good place to carve out a home, due to its geographical position halfway between the Red Sea and the Dead Sea. This simple fact soon put Petra on the map, becoming the crossroads that united Egypt, Arabia and Persia during the Ancient Greek and Roman times, when it was also a key caravan route for China's Silk Road, India's Spice Road and Arabia's Incense Road. The city was a busy, thriving centre of commerce as well as worship. But for some reason it was abandoned and became hidden from the world. Empty for centuries, it was not until the early 1900s that it was "discovered", reputedly by a European explorer who disguised himself in native costume to gain entry to the empty kingdom of rock.

Today, Petra's spiritual side is preserved in the world-famous rock-cut sites that boast its connection to its royal ancestors and important leaders – burial sites of more than 1,000 tombs spread over a distance of 264 square kilometres (102 sq. miles). Each tomb has a facade carved out of pink sandstone rock, behind which resides an inner chamber or a temple, where pilgrims would come to pay their respects. The most famous tomb, of course, is al-Khazneh, also known as the Treasury. This world-famous site is more than 2,000 years old and is believed to be the resting place of King Aretas IV, buried here in the 1st century CE, and whose daughter was married to the son of King Herod, the marriage that famously caused John the Baptist to lose his head.

Other nearby tombs of note are the Urn Tomb, which belonged to the Nabataean King Malchus II, who died in 70 CE, and the al-Deir Monastery, the second most visited building in Petra after al-Khazneh. These tombs are some of the most photographed spiritual sites in the world and locations of colossal sanctity to the classical world.

The entire area, the Petra Archaeological Park, was named one of the new seven wonders of the world.

Opposite: The word Petra, naturally, is derived from the Greek word *petros* or "rocks". Historians agree that less than 15 per cent of Petra's true size has been discovered, with the rest hidden, for now, under rock and key.

Prambanan Temple

A HINDU HOLY TRINITY UNITES IN INDONESIA

- ✷ Indonesia
- ✝ Hindu
- 🏛 856 CE
- 👥 2 million
- 📅 May–October
- 🗺 40 hectares (99 acres)

7°45′8″ S 110°29′30″ E

Prambanan Temple is a colossal compound built to honour the holy trinity (Trimūrti) of Hinduism: the Creator (Brahma), the Preserver (Vishnu) and the Destroyer (Shiva). It is the largest Hindu structure in Indonesia, and second only to Angkor Wat in terms of largest religious structures on earth.

A sprawling temple complex that is made up of 240 temples and a further 500 smaller shrines and monuments scattered about the site, this Indonesian national cultural icon was recognized by the UNESCO World Cultural Heritage in 1991. And not surprisingly.

Built under the orders of King Balitung Maha Sambu, ruler of Java's Kingdom of Mataram, as an architectural riposte to Borobudur, a mighty construction built by a rival Buddhist dynasty in Thailand (*see* page 22), only 50 kilometres (30 miles) away. Both sites are spiritual giants of their respective Hindu and Buddhist religions in the region, reflected in the tall and pointed artichoke-shaped stupas.

After construction, King Balitung Maha Sambu used Prambanan as his royal temple, conducting religious ceremonies to please the Hindu holy family and even, the legends state, human sacrifices. But it was for unknown reasons that the entire temple compound was abandoned 80 years after it had been completed, leaving the temples to be consumed by nature. Everything was left as it lay after several earthquakes reduced much of it to rubble. It was not until the 1930s that a restoration attempt of the main temples began, and it is still ongoing today. More importantly, after centuries of spiritual abandonment, the temples have been reclaimed as an important religious centre for Hindus.

The main star of Prambanan is the central compound, where eight main temples come together. This is the largest temple dedicated to Shiva, the destroyer and the restorer. The peak of this structure rises to a height of 47 metres (154 ft). Inside the temple, a statue of a four-armed Shiva, standing on Buddhist-style lotus blossoms, welcomes visitors looking to meditate and honour the deity. Made from basalt (lava) rock from the nearby Mount Merapi volcano, the temple includes parapets adorned with carvings of *Ramayana*, the ancient Sanskrit epic that tells the true story of Prince Rama's quest to rescue his beloved wife Sita from the clutches of Ravana with the help of an army of monkeys.

In November 2019, a sacred ceremony known as the *Abhiṣeka* was performed at the temple for the first time in more than 1,000 years. The *Abhiṣeka* cleansed, sanctified and purified the temple, restoring it to its original function as a focus of Hindu religious activity and distancing it from a simple tourist attraction. Indonesian Hindus believe that this ceremony marked a turning point to re-consecrate the temple grounds and to restore the spiritual energy of Prambanan Temple.

Opposite: Prambanan Temple city is breathtaking in its scale and stature and a spectacle to shock and awe one's spiritual senses. The site is surrounded by large fields and dense jungle canopies.

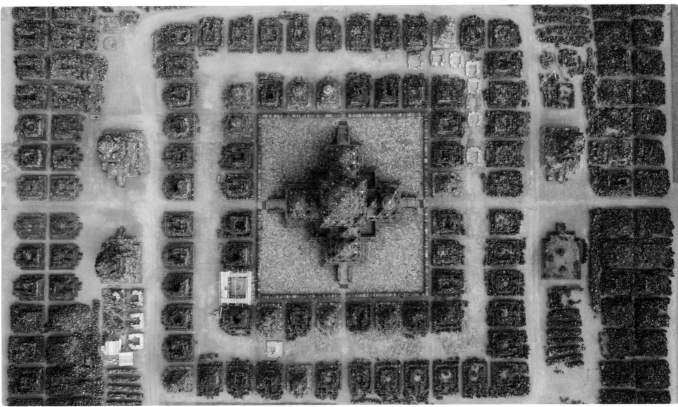

Pyramids of Giza

TOMBS TO TRANSPORT THE SPIRIT OF ANCIENT KINGS TO THE AFTERLIFE

⊛ Egypt

✝ Ancient Egyptian

⊓ 2570 BCE

👥 15 million

📅 November–March

📍 5.3 hectares (13 acres)

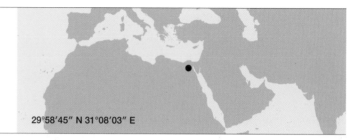

29°58′45″ N 31°08′03″ E

Three is a magic number. The Ancient Egyptians knew it. And although there are more than 100 pyramids scattered about the edges of Egypt's Western Desert, the Big Three in Giza are still the kings of ancient world wonder.

A mere 13 kilometres (8 miles) southwest of Cairo sit the Pyramids of Giza, unarguably the most iconic landmark of the classical world, and the first of the ancient wonders to be inscribed on the UNESCO World Heritage List in 1979. After more than 4,500 years they're still standing: they are the oldest surviving man-made monuments on earth. They were built to endure eternity, and they've yet to disappoint.

The three pyramids of Giza were created for three kings, or pharaohs. The largest, the Great Pyramid, was for King Khufu; the middle-sized pyramid, King Khafre; and the smallest, King Menkaure. All were built within a century of each other to honour the legacies of the power and authority of the bodies buried within. It was also a plan to inspire awe in the importance of kingship as far as the eyes can see.

Many theories abound on the spiritual significance of the pyramids, but archaeologists are certain that the three pyramids were built primarily as royal tombs of idolized pharaohs. The large granite coffins inside each pyramid were built first and then the pyramid and tomb rooms were constructed around the central coffin. However, the pyramids were more than just mausoleums. According to Egyptian mythology, they served as vessels to send the spirit of the kings, the *ka*, into the stars above, the afterlife, or Aaru – heaven – where the gods, such as the sun god Ra or Osiris, god of the underworld, live happily ever after.

For decades, astronomers wondered if the apex of the pyramid pointed to a particular star or constellation, or if it was a reflection of the Duat, the realm of the dead in ancient Egyptian mythology, which is represented in hieroglyphs as a three-pointed star encased in a circle. The three pyramids represent the three stars in Orion's Belt, the Great Sphinx belongs to the constellation Leo, and the Nile corresponds to the Milky Way, forming the three stars in a circle. However, this theory has been disputed.

The Ancient Egyptians believed the shape of a pyramid represented the descending rays of the sun, especially as seen in shadows on a sundial (an invention from Ancient Egypt). Once upon a time, each of the Pyramids of Giza was covered with a white limestone top layer, which was polished so that it would reflect the sun's rays and be almost blinding to look at. It was a great way to get the attention of Ra.

At the centre of the necropolis is the Great Pyramid, arguably the most iconic of the pyramids. It stands at 147 metres (482 ft) tall and took over 20 years to build. For 3,800 years, it was the largest man-made structure on earth, using more than two million limestone blocks and built by more than 100,000 skilled labourers – rather than slaves as once thought.

Opposite: All the pyramids of Egypt, including the three at Giza, are situated on the west bank of the Nile. It is where the sun sets every evening, which is also a symbol of a pharaoh's journey from life to the realm of the dead.

Sigiriya

FOLLOW THE PATH OF THE LION TO AN ANCIENT ROCK FORTRESS

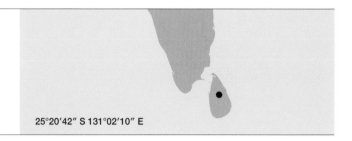

✳ Sri Lanka	◉ 1 million
✝ Buddhist	◷ January–March
⌷ 477 CE	⌖ 349 metres (1,145 ft) (height)

25°20′42″ S 131°02′10″ E

Rising from a steaming forest in Sri Lanka is Sigiriya – the "lion rock" – is described as the most valuable historical monument in the country. It is an ancient settlement built 1,500 years ago for one of the island state's most influential kings. This geological, historical and spiritual wonder still stands proud today and is a must-see for visitors.

Long established as a site in the UNESCO list of World Heritage Sites, Sigiriya – a monolithic rock pillar – rises from the surrounding forests looking more like a man-made statue or a beautiful artistic monument to a great leader than the site of a well-planned, ancient royal city. But it was here that a small city was built, reaching some 180 metres (600 ft) into the clouds from the plains below.

Planned by the royal leader himself, and built at the order and supervision of King Kashyapa I, this well fortified city was the capital of the local region until the defeat of the king around 495 CE. The site was subsequently used by Buddhist monks, who traditionally like to locate themselves in high, remote places for their strict meditation routines. But even the Buddhist monks ceased to use the rock some time around the 15th century, maybe moving across to the temples located in and around Pidurangala Rock, which is only 3 kilometres (1.8 miles) across the valley floor. The temple at the foot of Pidurangala is still in use even now.

Also still preserved today are the enormous carved paws of the lion that was the symbol of the hill city at the time. Visitors pass directly through them on their ascent up the rock to the summit, where the palace-cum-fortress city is located.

Mounting the 1,200 steps in the footsteps of the king leads to the most beautiful, tranquil scene, for not only is the top of the rock a well-planned complex, with a vast array of buildings, stairways and concourses, it was also home to a beautiful series of carefully constructed gardens, which featured an irrigation system that was way ahead of its time. Not finding enough water on the top (naturally), there was an incredibly advanced hydraulic system in place that still works today, attracting visitors from all over the world to wonder not only at the natural beauty of the rock but also the ingenuity of the native population of the time. Described as a "masterpiece of physics and engineering", modern archaeologists (and garden designers) are still fascinated by the advanced standard of planning and construction that ensured water was able to flow up, down and across to the gardens.

The walls of the rock are adorned with many colourful frescoes, although it is thought that the entire western face of the rock would have been covered in them originally. Unfortunately many of the frescoes are fading, although steps are being taken to slow down this natural process.

Opposite: The most impressive viewing point – and favourite for savvy tourists – is the nearby Pidurangala Rock. This neighbouring rock has an active Buddhist temple at the base, a ruined one in a series of caves near the top, and offers the best view of Sigiriya for miles around.

Skellig Islands

HAVENS OF TRANQUILLITY RISING FROM THE DEPTHS OF THE ATLANTIC OCEAN

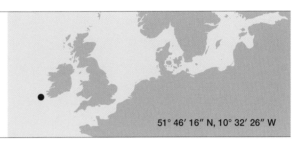

✺ Ireland

✝ Christian

🏛 588 CE

👥 15,000

🗓 May–September

📍 0.22 km² (0.08 sq. mi.) (Skellig Michael)

51° 46′ 16″ N, 10° 32′ 26″ W

In 2017, the Skelligs were used as the home of the Jedi temple and Luke Skywalker, The Last Jedi, in the blockbuster Star Wars franchise. For many, that's about as spiritual as a place can get. The spiritual force is strong with this one.

Before *Star Wars*, of course, the Skellig Islands were a world-renowned landmark surrounded by seabirds, spiritual ceremonies and stone temples, and the most westerly sacred site in Europe. The two islands, Skellig Michael (Great Skellig) and Little Skellig, rose out of the Atlantic Ocean around 360 million years ago, 12 kilometres (7 miles) off the coast of Ireland's southwestern tip of County Kerry. Today, it's a magical sight to behold from the sea and land at sunset and sunrise. It is also a safe haven for its native seabird, the puffin, and more than 50,000 of them – the second largest colony in the world – meet to mate.

Skellig Michael, with its twin pinnacles, was famous for its early Christian monastery, dating back to around 588 CE. The monks left some time around 1100, due to the remoteness and steepness of the jagged crags – there are 600 steep rocky steps to the top. Christian pilgrims and movie fans who make the journey by boat are sure to leave in awe at the fact that stone oratories and huts are still there, and in remarkable condition. This is despite adverse weather, which means the island is only accessible and hospitable during the summer months.

In 1996, UNESCO added Skellig Michael to the World Heritage List, citing it as a "unique example of an early religious settlement deliberately sited on a pyramidal rock in the ocean, preserved because of a remarkable environment". The island's remote, isolated location and inhospitable landscape – and to preserve the ruins of the once-great spiritual home – means only 180 people are allowed to set foot onto Skellig Michael per day; numbers are monitored carefully.

Tourists that are lucky enough to make it onto the Skelligs – and mother nature herself does not make it easy, with ferries often cancelled because of bad weather, and the famous lack of jetty means a leap of faith for the committed traveller only – soon get a feel for how remote the islands are. There is no gift shop, no information bureau and certainly no toilets. Visiting is more like a workout than a contemplative session, and although 600 steps may not sound like many, they are often slippery, are always steep and the only way down is the way you just came up. If you are lucky you may be able to steal a solitary moment in a shelter to ponder the wind, water and bird sounds.

However, it is no doubt that the destination remains "the spiritual adventure at the end of the material world", a place where solitude and a spiritual connection to the earth exist in abundance. Or, as Irish playwright George Bernard Shaw once famously said of these rocks, "I tell you the thing does not belong to any world that you and I have lived and worked in: it is part of our dream world."

Opposite: The word Skellig comes from the old Gaelic word sceillec, which means "a splinter of stone". Even travelling between the two islands is difficult.

Stonehenge

ENGLAND'S ANCIENT SPIRITUAL HOME, STILL SHROUDED IN SECRETS

⊛ England

✝ Pagan/Christian

🏛 2500 BCE

👥 1 million

📅 Summer Solstice (21 June)

🗺 26 km² (10 sq. mi.)

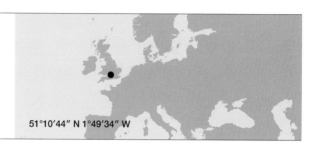

51°10′44″ N 1°49′34″ W

Stonehenge, a horseshoe-shaped stone structure protruding from the Salisbury Plains in Wiltshire, was a labour of love, and death, for late-Neolithic humans.

Much has been written about this amazing, world-famous UNESCO heritage site, and yet there remains plenty still to be revealed. The monument remains an enigma at the centre of Great Britain's ancient past, an icon of prehistoric engineering.

For some, Stonehenge is a spectacular spiritual centrepoint, where healing earth energies and ley lines align. Others agree with the local folklore: Stonehenge was created by King Arthur's wizard, Merlin, who magically transported the giant stones from Ireland. Others believe the stone alignment is a landing zone for future (past?) alien spacecraft. As with all legends, the truth is what you choose to believe... but there is one thing everyone does agree on: there is something deeply spiritual about the site.

After centuries of analysis and discovery, most historians and scientists today believe that Stonehenge was part holy site and part astronomical calendar, working in harmony with the sun and stars, and allowing the dwellers of the ditch to chart the movements of the sun through the year and carry out religious rituals in their honour. Indeed, the ruins align perfectly with the sunrise for summer solstice.

What is known, scientifically, is that around 5,000 years ago, a *henge* (a spherical ditch with an inner and an outer bank) was formed by human hand. About 500 years later, massive standing stones – each around 4 metres (13 ft) high, 2 metres (7 ft) wide and weighing 25 tonnes (24 tons) – were transported (it's unsure precisely how). The addition of the stones to the henge most likely took hundreds of years.

Stonehenge is created from two particular, and curious, types of stone. The larger, vertical stones are a sarsen sandstone. It is believed they were transported – magically or otherwise – from the Marlborough Downs, some 32 kilometres (20 miles) away. These stones have been sculpted and polished to appear bright. The sarsens are erected in two concentric configurations, an inner horseshoe and an outer circle. The smaller stones are bluestones (when they're wet they appear dark blue). These bluestones came from the Preseli Hills in western Wales, more than 240 kilometres (150 miles) away. To this day, geologists cannot confirm why the builders of Stonehenge used these particular stones, though the blue hue certainly is a big clue; the ancient builders perhaps credited them with healing powers.

On the summer solstice, 21 June, the sun rises slightly to the left of the Heel Stone – the largest of the stone blocks – which weighs more than 30 tonnes (29 tons). At the winter solstice, the sun drops down directly above the Altar Stone – a sandstone block – before disappearing from view.

Scientists, spiritualists, conspiracists and tourists – all are drawn to Stonehenge, and the Stonehenge World Heritage Site – which contains more than just the legendary stone circle – covering an area seven-and-a-half times larger than Manhattan's Central Park.

Opposite: Inside the henge, more than 60 cremated bodies were unearthed, meaning Stonehenge is also the largest late-Neolithic cemetery in the country.

Ubud

SPIRITUAL CENTRE FOR ENLIGHTENMENT AND ESCAPE FOR WORLD EXPLORERS

⊛ Indonesia

† Balinese Hindu

🏛 300 BCE

👥 3 million

📅 All year round

📍 42 km² (16 sq. mi.)

56.0152° N, 23.4153° E

Surrounded by jungles of beautiful banyan trees and terraced mountainside rice paddies is where you'll find Bali's ancient village, Ubud, a sought-after destination famed for its Hindu shrines, spiritual retreats and centuries-long (virtually) unspoiled serenity.

Ubud, in Balinese, means medicine, and this idyllic island community is, indeed, famed among foreigners from far-flung places and locals as a place rich in mystical healing powers, as well as revered as a modern Mecca for those seeking mediation, and medication, for the soul. There are also plenty of ancient religious relics to be found, and more than 3,000,000 new age spiritual tourists, digital nomads and yoga students seek serenity and wellness in Ubud's *shalas* every year. That is more than half of Bali's annual visitors, and more than enough to ensure Ubud merits its title as Bali's beating cultural, artistic and spiritual heart.

Many hundreds of years ago, as far back as the 8th century, a local legend tells of Bali's royal families sending their sickly relatives to Ubud in order to be healed by the village's myriad of mystical and magical healers, the descendants of whom can still be found in the village today dispensing traditional and herbal medicines for all that ails; old customs endure the test of time.

Ubud's standout ancient spiritual attraction is perhaps the Gunung Lebah Temple (mountain valley temple) that was founded by the Javanese Hindu priest Rsi Markendya, who first began to meditate at this precise spot at the confluence of two rivers, a spiritually significant feature for Hindus. It was Markendya who founded and oversaw the construction of Ubud's major temples, offering a home to 90 per cent of the roughly 12,000 population that practices Balinese Hinduism. Most of the rest of Indonesia is Muslim. It is this unique religious practice that ensures Ubud

remains special and why, everywhere you look, Balinese Hindu females leave offerings of brightly coloured frangipani flowers at the entrance of the temples. This is a spiritual tradition known as *Canang sari*, a praise and prayer to Sang Hyang Widhi Wasa, the supreme god of Indonesian Hinduism.

Every 210 days – or one year, in the Balinese Pakuwon calendar – Ubud's entire community, regardless of faith, observes Pagerwesi, the day of wisdom, and comes together to cleanse and strengthen their minds and souls and to ensure Ubud remains a place free from evil spirits. The two other important holidays in the Balinese calender are Soma Ribek – celebrated the week before Pagerwesi – a day dedicated to Bhatari Sri, the goddess of rice. The other is Sabuh Mas, the Tuesday before, when worship of the god Siva as a wealth giver is observed.

Although visitors are encouraged, there are a number of rules to be observed by tourists if they do wish to visit the temples. As well as the basics, like wearing a scarf or sarong and covering up shoulders, it is considered improper to wear shoes in a temple and the direction of feet is important – pointing directly at a shrine with feet, seen as unclean, can be considered rude.

Opposite: Overgrown, atmospheric and other-worldly, Ubud reached a new zenith as the spiritual hotspot of Bali with the release of the global bestselling book and film *Eat Pray Love*, in 2006 and 2010 respectively.

Wat Chaiwatthanaram

THE ORIGINAL SPIRITUAL JEWEL IN THE THAI KINGDOM'S CROWN

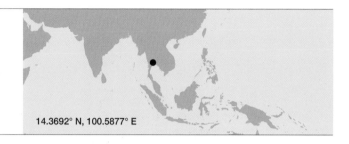

- ⊛ Ayutthaya, Thailand
- ✝ Theravada Buddhist
- ▥ 1350
- ⍟ 2 million
- ▥ November–April
- ⊕ 2.9 km² (1.1 sq. mi.)

14.3692° N, 100.5877° E

The "invincible city" of Ayutthaya flourished for four centuries before it was almost decimated from memory. It is the home of the mighty Wat Chaiwatthanaram, long considered Thailand's most spiritually sacred site.

It was founded by King Ramathibodi, the first king of the Ayutthaya Kingdom, the precursor to modern Thailand, in 1350, at the confluence of three major rivers: Chao Phraya, Lop Buri and Pa Sak. Ayutthaya was one of the world's first, and largest, commerce and government capitals, as well as being a sanctuary and haven for monks and Theravada Buddhists. Both would pilgrimage there for the two main festivals in the Buddhist calendar, Wesak and Parinirvana Day, as well as for spiritual retreats in the name of contemplation and reflection.

Today, however, Ayutthaya is little more than an archaeological site, albeit a vast, stunning one. All that endures are the remains of tall *prangs* (towers with a spire) and Buddhist monasteries, the size and stature of which indicate just how civilized and impressive this city once was, and the grand designs its architects had. Ayutthaya was conquered by the Burmese army in 1767, which razed it to the ground, and forced its inhabitants to flee into the forests, never to return. The city was never rebuilt.

At the heart of Ayutthaya is its Historical Park, a UNESCO site, and its shining star: Wat Chaiwatthanaram, a major pilgrimage site for the nation's 60 million Theravada Buddhists. It is considered by cultural historians as the structure that best defines Buddhism's influence on Thai society and it is magnificent.

Construction was ordered in 1630 by King Prasat Thong, first of his dynasty, and the temple's name translates as the "Temple of long reign and glorious era". The temple was constructed over a 20-year period, which was seen as a relatively long time frame in that part of the world at that time. Stories attribute the temple to be a memorial for the king's mother, as some upheaval was going on around the time of her death, leading to a change in regime; the new ruler respected his elder.

The main tower of the central temple is surrounded by four smaller prangs and hundreds of gilded Buddha image statues – identical to the architectural style of the Angkor Wat temple in Cambodia that had been built half a century earlier. Also as in Angkor Wat, each tower at Wat Chaiwatthanaram symbolizes Mount Meru, the five-peak golden mountain, and the centre of all the physical, metaphysical and spiritual universes held scared in Hindu and Buddhist cosmology.

Around the walls of the temple are relief sculptures that tell the story of the Buddha's life, and although weather has taken a toll they are still interesting. The inside walls have many paintings on them, too. Much of the site is crumbly, and somewhat weather beaten, but it has survived the humidity, attacks and various other adverse conditions, and remains one of the most deeply spiritual locations in the world.

Opposite: Wat Chaiwatthanaram central spire spikes the sky at 35 metres (115 ft) tall, allowing it be seen for miles – a shining beacon to Buddhists everywhere.

CHAPTER 2

Places
of Worship

Organized religion has been with us for millennia, and the golden era of palace-like churches, incredible mosques and buildings capable of holding huge congregations looks to continue for a long time. This chapter looks at some of the largest, most important and significant sites that have drawn crowds of the devoted for thousands of years.

Aachen Cathedral

CHARLEMAGNE'S SPIRITUAL HOME AWAY FROM ROME

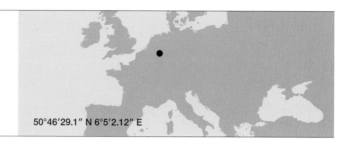

- ✳ Germany
- ✝ Roman Catholic
- 🏛 805 CE
- 👥 1 million
- 📅 All year round
- 🗺 2,000 m² (21,530 sq. ft)

50°46'29.1" N 6°5'2.12" E

In 1978, Aachen Cathedral became one of the first 12 locations to be listed as a UNESCO World Heritage site, because of its "world importance, and as one of the great examples of church architecture." Making such history would have brought immense satisfaction to the legendary Emperor Charlemagne.

To know the spiritual significance of Aachen Cathedral is to learn the history of one of the most important and significant European rulers, Charlemagne – or Charles the Great. King of the Franks and emperor of the west between 800 CE and 814 CE, Charlemagne was the first Roman Emperor to be considered "holy" (this title was bestowed upon him when he as crowned *Imperator Romanorum* by Pope Leo III himself). Charlemagne's actions not only boosted Europe's economic fortune but also ushered in a whole new cultural revival (known as the Carolingian Renaissance) that saw, for example, great works of ancient art saved for posterity. It was the first of such revivals in centuries.

Charlemagne lived, worshipped and died at the palace-cum-cathedral that he devised himself. The ruler was present at its inception in 796 CE and his body was interred there in 814 CE. His ambition with the cathedral was to create a new version of the Roman Empire, and Aachen Cathedral was to be the shining place of worship at the centre of his new domain. He considered Aachen to be important geographically for its proximity to the border with the Netherlands and Belgium, and it was strategically placed in the centre of his family's territory.

His ambition for construction was as lofty as the completed cathedral itself, a structure that spikes 72 metres (236 ft) into the skyline. After Charlemagne's passing, and from 900 CE to 1500,

the cathedral was *the* sacred site of coronation for more than 31 German kings and 12 queens, a fact that ensured the cathedral remained at the centre of world politics for a further six centuries.

The impressive octagonal dome on top was shaped in this way because of Charlemagne's spiritual fascination with the numeral eight. (An octagon can be drawn using two intersecting squares within a circle; the circle represents God's eternity while the square represents the secular world – Charlemagne saw himself as the ruler of both the religious and secular worlds). It is believed to have been built in just ten years, a wonder of early medieval engineering, if true.

Aachen Cathedral, like Charlemagne bringing together the religious and secular worlds, unified architectural forms from the eastern and western parts of his empire, ensuring that this sacred site felt inclusive for anyone who visited, and one of the key reasons it is a major site for religious and non-religious visitors even today. Inside the building there is a wealth of treasures, relics and art saved from Charlemagne's time, making the structure as much a fascinating museum as an ancient place of worship.

Opposite: Extensive exterior renovations were started in 1986 and completed by 2011 as part of an overall renovation of the entire cathedral that encompassed remedial works as well as preservation for the future.

Al Farooq Omar Bin Al Khattab Mosque

DIVINE DEVOTION TO MUHAMMAD'S MOST TRUSTED DISCIPLE

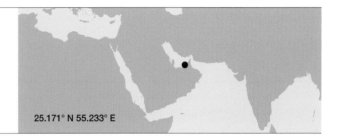

✱ United Arab Emirates	👥 N/A
✝ Islam	📅 All year round
🏛 1986	📍 4.2 km² (1.6 sq. mi.)

25.171° N 55.233° E

The Mosque is Dubai's largest centre of devotion to Islam, and a place of worship and wonder for pilgrims – spiritual and secular. It is a destination that promotes ancient virtues of faith and builds bridges between Arabic civilization and other religions.

Mosques are sacred spaces for the teaching and practicing of Islamic faith rituals, traditions, rules and etiquette. They bring the brotherhood of Islam together, allowing the bond of all Muslims to grow as one. Omar Bin Al Khattab, one of the ten companions of the prophet Muhammad, took this belief seriously, and this is why he was given the sacred designation *Al Farooq*, meaning the "one who distinguishes right from wrong". This magnificent mosque takes its divine inspiration from Omar.

Like the 12 disciples of Christ, the 10 companions of Muhammad – the divinely inspired prophet and 7th-century founder of Islam – were revered as *al-ashara al-mubashsharūn* – the "ten to whom Paradise was promised". Omar was so revered he was buried next to Muhammad at the sacred site of Al-Masjid an-Nabawi, Medina, Saudi Arabia, following his assassination in November 644 CE. In Islam today, Omar is kept close as one of the most important caliphs – a successor of Muhammad's teachings – in promoting the virtues of the Islamic faith. Omar's mosque is one of the UAE's largest and was one of the first in the world to allow entry to non-Muslims.

In tandem with its sacred ancestry, the structure itself is incredibly impressive. In accordance with Islamic architectural style, there are four minarets that are 65 metres (213 ft) tall. In Arabic, *minaret* means "beacon", and it is the tower from which the faithful are called to prayer five times each day. In addition, there are 21 domes, with 124 stained-glass windows designed in a way "inspired by the Ottoman style of building minarets with conic endings like a sharp pencil" and scores of intricate interior details that contribute to making this place supremely special, including walls that are engraved with bright Arabic calligraphy of inscribed Quranic verses.

As is common with mosques, Muslims must enter for prayers with the right leg first, saying the holy words, *Bismillah, Allahumma Salli Ala Muhammad, Allahumma-iftah li Abwaba Rahmatik* ("In the name of Allah, and prayers and peace be upon the Messenger of Allah. O Allah, open the gates of Your mercy for me.") and then exit with the left leg first, saying *Allahumma Salli `Ala Muhammad, Allahumma Inni As'aluka min Fadlik* ("In the name of Allah, and prayers and peace be upon the Messenger of Allah. O Allah, I ask You from Your favour)."

Opposite: The Islamic architectural style of the mosque – the mihrab, the minbar and the four minarets – is inspired by the famous Blue Mosque in Istanbul, Turkey (which itself was inspired by the Hagia Sophia, *see page 78*).

Al-Masjid an-Nabawi

THE PROPHET MUHAMMAD'S FINAL HOME UNDER THE GREEN DOME

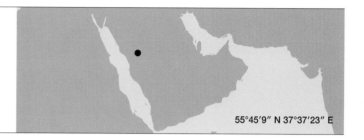

- (✴) Saudi Arabia
- (✝) Islam
- (🏛) 623 CE
- (👥) 14 million
- (📅) 2 August
- (📍) 8.2 hectares (20 acres)

55°45′9″ N 37°37′23″ E

Al-Masjid an-Nabawī, in the holy city of Medina, is the size of a city. But its size is equalled only by its spiritual power. It is the second holiest site in all of Islam, after the Masjid al-Haram in Mecca, (*see* page 110) and the second largest mosque in the world. And there's more…

Al-Masjid an-Nabawī, translated into English means "The Prophetic Mosque", and for good reason. It was built by the prophet Muhammad, the founding father of Islam, who spent his divinely inspired life preaching the teachings of Adam, Abraham, Moses and Jesus here. Due to its connection to Muhammad, the mosque has been expanded to house one million pilgrims at the same time, making it easily one of the largest pilgrimage sites in the world. It is simply huge, and worthy of a visit in person.

The large mosque complex we see today, with its ten iconic minarets, is 100 times the size of the original mosque Muhammad built when he founded Islam more than 1,500 years ago. That original mosque took him roughly eight months to build, and he was indeed involved heavily in its construction. (It was the second mosque built by Muhammad in Medina, after his original, the Quba Mosque, which still stands today.)

Underneath the iconic Green Dome (it hasn't always been green, having been changed from purple-blue about 150 years ago), in the southeast corner of the mosque lies the tomb of Muhammad himself. Following the mosque's completion, Muhammad read the Friday sermon every week until his death ten years later, on 8 June, 632 CE. This was approximately three months after his famous and final pilgrimage to Mecca some 482 kilometres (300 miles) away.

The mosque, as built by Muhammad, was said to be approximately 30 metres (100 ft) by 35 metres (117 ft) and was only around 3.6 metres (11 ft 10 in.) high. That mosque was expanded regularly for thousands of years, notably under Rashidun caliph Uthman, who was responsible for demolishing the original mosque in 649 CE. The new mosque was much larger than the original, and made of stone, iron and mortar, as well as wood.

Less than 100 years later, the mosque was renovated over a three-year period and the size increased considerably once more. The style became a lot more decorative and minarets were added for the first time. The mosque continued to be expanded and improved a number of times, and in 1837 a new dome was constructed that was subsequently painted green. This was the first time the mosque was referred to as *Kubbe-i Khadra* ("the green dome").

Inside the mosque are various beautifully decorated elements, including two mihrabs (a niche that indicates the direction of Mecca), one of which is decorative (and built by Muhammad himself), the other fully functional and set in marble. An ornate gold minbar (where the imam stands to deliver a sermon) is another significant sight.

Opposite: In 1909, the mosque was the first place in all of Arabia to have electricity.

Church of the Holy Sepulchre

LOCATIONS OF CHRIST'S LAST FEW HOURS ON EARTH, ALL UNDER ONE ALMIGHTY ROOF

- ✳ Israel
- ✝ Christian
- 🏛 326 CE
- 👥 4 million
- 📅 April–May; Sept–Oct
- 📍 0.5 hectares (1.2 acres)

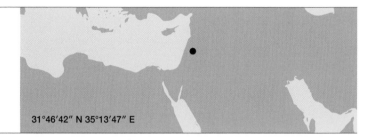

31°46′42″ N 35°13′47″ E

For the world's 2.4 billion followers of the New Testament, this church is the holy trinity of spiritual places – it occupies the crucifixion, burial and resurrection sites of Jesus Christ.

The Church of the Holy Sepulchre has a history that dates back almost as long as the legacy of Christ. Located in the northwest quarter of the Old City of Jerusalem, the church has been destroyed twice (burned down in 614 CE and destroyed in 1009), but thankfully it was also restored both times. And the last time it was restored, it was made twice as big in the process.

In 312 CE, the Roman ruler Constantine the Great reported that he had seen a vision in the sky. It was of a burning cross and is commonly believed to be one of the factors that led him to become the first emperor to convert to Christianity. In 325 CE, Constantine sent his mother, Helena, on a quest to Jerusalem to find Christ's burial tomb following his Crucifixion. Helena found it right here, after learning details of a particular rock-cut tomb which was said could cure the living from becoming dead, as well as being the one that housed the "True Cross" that Jesus had been crucified on. Within a year, a shrine had been built that enclosed the tomb walls within its own. Ever since Helena's discovery it has been a vitally important pilgrimage for followers of Christ. Christians believe that after Jesus rose from the dead here in his tomb, he did not die a second time. Instead, 40 days after his resurrection, the son of God left the earth by ascending to heaven, leaving behind no final resting place in the history books.

According to the Bible, John 19:41–42, Jesus's burial and resurrection place, or "empty" tomb, was close to his place of Crucifixion, which was known as "the Hill of Calvary", from the Latin *calvaria*, meaning "skull", translated from the Greek *golgotha*, meaning "place of skull"). This is where Jesus's hands were nailed to the cross, and so the church enclosed the site of both. The word "sepulchre" translates as "tomb". Inside the tomb lies a massive slab of marble where, it is said, Christ's body was laid to rest. The church also houses the Chapel of the Crowning of the Thorns, the place where Christ's walk to his Crucifixion site at the top of the hill began, as well as the place where the Crown of Thorns was placed on Christ's head.

Located between the Hill of Calvary and Jesus's tomb is the Stone of Unction, or the Rock of Golgotha, which is a large stone in which Jesus's body was laid and prepared for burial. It was anointed with spices and wrapped in cloth before being placed inside the tomb. The rock is covered by glass, but pilgrims can touch the rock with their hand by uncovering a small opening. It is said to give goosebumps to even non-believers.

Opposite: The church complex is large, roughly the same size as an American football pitch.

Church of the Nativity

ON THIS SPOT A SPECIAL CHILD WAS BORN IN BETHLEHEM

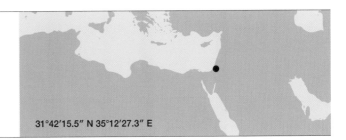

- ✳ Palestine
- ✝ Christian
- ⛩ 326 CE
- 👥 2.5 million
- 📅 March–May; Sept–Nov
- 📍 1.2 km² (.4 sq. mi.)

31°42'15.5" N 35°12'27.3" E

Underneath the altar, down two staircases and through a network of caves is a locked door. Behind this door is the Nativity Grotto, the cave where 15 silver lamps shine a light on the star that marks the spot where Mary gave birth to a boy, the son of God, and Christianity's lord and saviour: Jesus.

This location is, perhaps, the most sacred of all spiritual sites in the Christian faith and the endpoint for the Nativity Pilgrimage, the 1,500-year-old ceremonial route that not only marks the beginnings of Christianity but also the holiest spot in Christendom for two billion followers. It is also sacred for the most widely celebrated religious festivity in the world: Christmas.

When, at Christmas time, carollers sing the hymn "Away in a manger/No crib for a bed/The little Lord Jesus/Laid down His sweet head", they are singing of here, the Church of the Nativity. It is 10 kilometres (6 miles) south of the old city of Jerusalem, in a once-small town called Bethlehem – and the precise spot where the Virgin Mary gave birth to her child, alongside Joseph.

Marking the floor where the newborn baby first made contact with the world is a 14-point silver star. It is inscribed in Latin with the words, *Hic De Virgine Maria Jesus Christus Natus Est – 1717* (Here Jesus Christ was born to the Virgin Mary – 1717). The points of the star represent each generation of Jesus Christ's ancestral genealogy, dating back to Abraham and Adam. In the centre of the star is a hole through which there is a stone that can be touched. This stone, it is said, is the one Mary laid down on as she gave birth to her son.

Over the centuries, this birthplace has grown from a manger to a cave to a basilica, the latter of which was commissioned by the Roman Emperor Constantine the Great, after his mother, Helena, made a pilgrimage here in 325 CE. She was so touched by the spiritual significance of this spot that she asked her son to build a church over the cave to ensure its protection. Indeed, the site survives almost untouched from its original construction and is now the oldest continuously used place of worship in Christianity, and the basilica is the oldest church in the Holy Land.

The Church of the Nativity is one of nine sacred places in Jerusalem and Bethlehem that are protected by a 250-year-old arrangement called the Status Quo. This is a firm understanding among the six Christian communities – Church of the East, Oriental Orthodoxy, Eastern Orthodoxy, Roman Catholicism, Protestantism, and Restorationism – with the aim of preserving the division of ownership and responsibilities of the nine sacred Christian holy places. The other eight sites are the Church of the Holy Sepulchre (*see* page 68), The Deir es-Sultan, the Tomb of the Virgin Mary, the Chapel of the Milk Grotto, the Chapel of the Shepherd's Field, the Chapel of the Ascension, the Western Wall (*see* page 122) and Rachel's Tomb.

Opposite: Since 2012, the Church of the Nativity is a UNESCO World Heritage Site. It was the first to be inscribed in Palestine.

Dome of the Rock

IMMORTAL FOOTPRINTS ENSHRINED IN STONE BENEATH A GOLDEN DOME

⚛ Israel

✝ Islam, Christian, Judaism

🏛 658 CE

👥 4.5 million

📅 All year round

📍 141,680 m² (169,447 sq. yd)

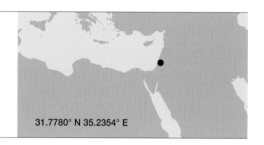

31.7780° N 35.2354° E

Welcome to Jerusalem, a super-spiritual destination where Islam and Judaism unite in relatively peaceful matrimony. The most enduring symbol of the city is, of course, the shrine at the top: the Dome of the Rock.

Here, the land beneath our feet is possessed and blessed by the Almighty, with much of its divine energies focused on the Dome of the Rock, located on the Temple Mount, or Haram al-Sharif as it is known to Muslims. This large octagonal-shaped shrine, which makes up roughly 20 per cent of the Old City's total surface area, is rated as the third most holy site in Islam, following Mecca and Al-Masjid an-Nabawī, Medina.

Known in Arabic as *Qubbat as-Sakhrah*, the iconic golden dome at the centre of this deeply significant structure is a shining light, illuminating the path for hundreds of millions of pilgrims to come home – and it is the destination where all worldwide Islam and Judaism prayers are directed – as it has been for millennia. This beautiful structure, overwhelming in its purpose and message of divine devotion, is the oldest existing Islamic place of worship on earth. Its construction was ordered by Abd al-Malik ibn Marwan ibn al-Hakam, one of the first Muslims, as a shrine for Islamic pilgrims, as well as a symbol to boast Islam's fast rise to become a world religion 1,500 years ago, following Muhammad's divine master plan.

For those followers of Islam who attend to worship, the dome protects them from the elements in the exact spot where the Prophet Muhammad ascended unto heaven – an event known as his Miraj. According to the Quran, it is written that as Muhammad was lifted heavenwards holding the hand of the Archangel Gabriel, his footprint left an indentation in the stone

as he took flight, leaving an indelible mark that is still visible today; significant for many religious followers.

Of different significance, for Jewish and Christian disciples, the Dome is home to what they call the Foundation Stone, or the Noble Rock. It is here that marks the spot where Abraham – the first Jew and the embodiment of the Jewish peoples' preservation of God's commandments – stood when asked by God to sacrifice his son, Isaac. By asking him to sacrifice his son, God tested Abraham's trust and devotion to his new faith. Abraham agreed, believing God would then bring his son back from the dead. However, just as the father was about to sacrifice the son, Gabriel, God's highest angel, appeared to Abraham on the rock and said, "Now I know you fear God". Instead of his son, Abraham sacrificed a ram. It is Gabriel's handprint that the Jewish believe is indented on the rock. For Jews the Dome of the Rock is where God's divine presence manifests itself more than in any other place. For those who have visited, that deep-rooted spirituality certainly weighs on the senses; this is a place with an incredible history across multiple beliefs.

Opposite: Located within the Old City of Jerusalem, the Dome of the Rock is within walking distance of the Western Wall and the Church of the Holy Sepulchre, both also blessed with enormous spiritual significance.

Frauenkirche

DRESDEN'S DOME-SHAPED EMBLEM OF DEFIANCE

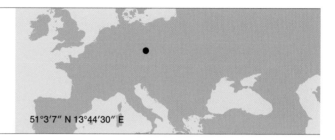

✳ Dresden, Germany

✝ Christian/Protestant

🏛 1726

🏃 2 million

📅 All year round

⛰ 91 metres (298 ft) (height)

51°3'7" N 13°44'30" E

Since its upscaling in 1726, Dresden Frauenkirche (Church of Our Lady) has been a towering symbol of faith, not only of humankind's affection for the Virgin Mary but also of defiance and resilience in the face of destruction.

A church has stood on the grounds of the Frauenkirche for more than 1,000 years. Its current, and most modern, incarnation is widely considered to be a pioneer of the architectural possibilities of the age – it is Baroque in style – and is a building that was brought to life by Dresden's famous city architect, George Bähr.

The Frauenkirche was completed in 1743, and its construction was paid for by the proudly Protestant city folk as an act of defiance towards the then Prince-elect, Frederick August I, who had converted to Catholicism in order to become King of Poland. Frederick approved the construction of the church, however, and reassured the people of Dresden that he would not impose *cuius regio, eius religio* ("whose realm, their religion") upon them. He foresaw that such an impressive architectural marvel would be beneficial to the fortunes of Dresden. Indeed, the church's dome, which is still one of the largest in Europe, soon became a world-famous symbol of the city.

Unlike the usual domes constructed for cathedrals of that time, which were often made from wood and covered with copper or lead, Bähr, uniquely, used local sandstone, allowing the church to stand out even more, as the sandstone turns darker as it ages. Atop the 23.5-metre (77-ft)-long stone dome sits a stone bell, or Steinernen Glocke, as it is known. At noon every day the church's bell rings aloud, giving the city's Protestant population – and everyone else – a moment to pause and pray.

On 15 February 1945, the church and its 12,000-tonne (11,810-ton)-dome collapsed completely due to the heavy bombings the city suffered, a result of the Allied retaliation during the latter stages of the Second World War. This was all the sadder, as the dome had previously survived a cannonball attack from the Prussian army during the Seven Years' War (1756–1763). As much as 50 per cent of the entire city was destroyed alongside the building of worship amid some of the most widespread aerial destruction in the entire conflict, and one that hastened the endgame.

Reborn from the ashes of that war, however, the Frauenkirche proved its resilience once more. It was reconstructed from the rubble using Bähr's original plans from 1726. The interior frescoes, mosaics, paintings and carved oak doors were also faithfully recreated, with old wedding photographs taken of couples on their happy day in times past proving to be very useful sources of reference. The golden cross on top of the church was made by a British goldsmith whose father was an Allied pilot in air raids over Dresden. The cross was the perfect symbol of reconciliation for this timeless church.

Opposite: Every January, the Frauenkirche closes its doors to the public and undergoes a mass cleaning operation of the giant Stone Bell as well as the church's interior.

Great Mosque of Djenné

MALI'S MASSIVE MUD MOSQUE, REMADE BY MUSLIMS AFTER THE MONSOON

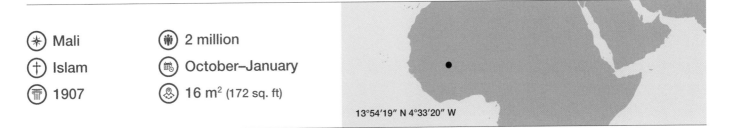

- ✳ Mali
- ✝ Islam
- 🏛 1907
- 👥 2 million
- 📅 October–January
- 📍 16 m² (172 sq. ft)

13°54'19" N 4°33'20" W

Mali's Great Mosque, found in Djenné – a UNESCO-protected southern town in the scorching-hot Sahara Desert – may be the world's largest mud-brick building. It is also the place of worship for 80 per cent of Mali's Muslims, as well as being the city's epicentre of religious and cultural life.

The walls of this magnificent mosque were first made of sun-baked earth bricks called *ferey* (and married together using a sand- and earth-based mortar) sometime in the 13th century under the orders of King Koi Konboro, Djenné's 26th ruler and first Muslim sultan. As an expression of his newfound faith, Konboro tore down his own palace and built the nation's first mosque in its place, using only local materials and traditional Islamic architectural techniques, such as conical minarets. For 600 years, this mud-built mosque was the centre of the town and soon the legend of its splendour spread as far and as wide as Europe and beyond.

Found between the floodplains of the Niger and Bani rivers and inhabited since 250 BCE, Djenné is one of the oldest cities in Western Africa. It is still the most populated, which is an important factor to consider, when every year the mosque needs to be more or less rebuilt by more than 4,000 plasterers and decorators. This is because of Mali's monsoon season, when the entire annual rainfall – more than 1,000mm (40 in.) – falls in just two months (July and August). This rainfall, naturally, takes its toll on the relatively unprotected walls of the Great Mosque.

Thankfully, the structure's exceptional hand-built construction is able to survive such an onslaught from the heavens. However, to ensure it stays strong from erosion and cracks for future generations, every April, during the dry season, a one-day traditional and religious renewal festival known as *Crepissage de la Grand Mosquée* (the "Plastering of the Great Mosque") occurs at the mosque. It is an event that unites the Muslim community as they carry out essential restoration work and renew the smooth layer of mud which covers the bricks. As the day-long plastering starts, so too does the prayer and celebrating of Djenné's community, faith and heritage. The night before, the town takes part in *La Nuit de Veille*, or the "Waking Night", a lively carnival in the moonlight, where prayer awakens the town at 4 a.m. to signal the beginning of the most important event on the calendar. For the whole month, the repair of the mosque is all that matters.

With its conical-spiral minarets that are typical of traditional Islam architectural style, the mosque is an enduring symbol of western Africa's religious devotion. The iconic wooden "spikes" – bundles of rodier palm sticks called *toron* – that emerge from the mud walls may look sinister, but in fact they help to ventilate and keep the structure stable. Each *toron* represents a verse from the Quran. This is truly a mosque unlike any other, and a fine monument to its devout creators.

Opposite: The mosque was completely rebuilt in 1907 following almost precisely the exact architecture of the original 13th-century design.

Hagia Sophia

THE SPIRITUAL HOME FOR MORE THAN 1.5 BILLION SOULS

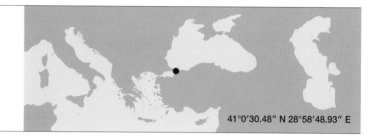

- ✴ Turkey
- ✝ Islam
- 🏛 360 BCE
- 👥 4 million
- 📅 November–March
- 🗺 1.8 hectares (4.5 acres)

41°0'30.48" N 28°58'48.93" E

Church. Cathedral. Mosque. Museum. For 1,600 years, Istanbul's Church of Holy Wisdom (Hagia Sophia), along the banks of the Bosporus Strait, has meant many things to millions of pilgrims, and across many faiths.

Above all of its complex history, religious tensions and cross-continental politics, the Hagia Sophia has, paradoxically, remained an enduring icon of spirituality, a hypnotic place dedicated to healing, peace and prosperity.

For 1,000 years, this enormous cathedral had the largest interior space in the world and was revered as the biggest religious centre of the Eastern Orthodox Church. There was, and still is, no place like it for pilgrims anywhere on earth. (Except, perhaps, the Blue Mosque, also in Istanbul. And while perhaps equally impressive, that other significant monument cannot match the Hagia Sophia's incredible, lengthy history.)

Built at the command of Roman Emperor Justinian I, and completed in 537 CE, the Hagia Sophia was the beating religious heart of the Byzantine Empire (the eastern faction of the Roman Empire), in the legendary city of Constantinople, before the capital's name was changed to Istanbul in 1453. It was aslso at that point that the cathedral underwent the conversion from Christianity to Islam, and became a mosque. And so it remained, until 1935 – all the while undergoing many interior transformations – before it was converted again, this time into a museum. This happened when Turkey became secular as part of its bid for modernization. But the story continues, and in 2020, the Hagia Sophia was once again reclassified as a mosque – Turkey has a majority Muslim population – to plenty of controversy worldwide.

Hagia Sophia remains the fascination of international reverence, thanks, in large part to being one of the rare structures in the world to have a circular dome on top of a square building, an architectural marvel known as a pendentive dome. The Hagia Sophia's dome is a representation of the realm of heaven, and is the second largest in the world – second only to the Pantheon in Rome. Soaring 55 metres (182 ft) high, with a diameter of 40 metres (131 ft), the dome's weight is supported by a series of smaller domes, arcades and four large arches.

Of course, from a spiritual perspective, the Hagia Sophia is highly recommended for believers of all faiths (or none!), and it has many facets that elevate the landmark above being more than just an architectural masterpiece, which it undoubtedly is as well. For example, in the northwest of the mosque, there is a "weeping" column (one of the 107 columns that hold the entire structure up) that is said to have healing powers. Curiously – and mysteriously – the pillar is damp to touch. It was blessed by Saint Gregory (Pope Gregory I, a former bishop of Rome) in the 15th century, and visitors can rub the wet column in the hope of being healed of whatever ails them.

Opposite (above): Hagia Sophia's famous four minarets were added when the landmark became a mosque. Below: Both Christian and Islamic religious elements are visible inside the colourful mosque.

Jasna Góra Monastery

A BEACON OF LIGHT FOR POLISH CATHOLICISM IN THE SPIRITUAL CAPITAL OF POLAND

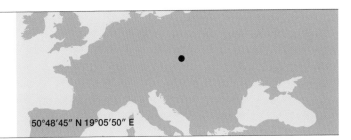

- ✳ Poland
- ✝ Roman Catholic
- 🏛 1382
- 👥 4.5 million
- 🗓 All year round
- 📍 106 m (347 ft) (height)

50°48′45″ N 19°05′50″ E

One of the top three largest Catholic pilgrimage sites in the world, Jasna Góra Monastery, atop Luminous Hill (Jasna Góra) in Czestochowa, is the home of St Luke's miraculous "Black Madonna", one of the most important icons of Christianity.

So famous is Jasna Góra Monastery that it was visited by Pope John Paul II every time he visited Poland. In August 1982, to celebrate the 600th anniversary of the arrival and veneration of the Black Madonna there, Pope John Paul II said of the artefact, "May the Lady of Jasna Góra win in us and through us! May she win even through our afflictions and defeats. May she ensure that we shall not desist from trying and struggling for truth and justice, for liberty and dignity in our lives." High praise, indeed.

Sitting atop the 293-metre (961-ft)-high "Luminous Hill", Jasna Góra is sacred ground to devout disciples of Christ and the Holy Family. It is a historic, iconic, fortress that protects the Black Madonna, Saint Luke's tabletop painting of the Virgin Mary holding the Infant Jesus. It is one of the first paintings ever recorded of the two, perhaps even dating back to a time both of them were alive together.

According to Christian tradition, it is believed that Saint Luke – one of the four evangelists of Christ, the writer of one of the gospels and the patron saint of artists – depicted the Virgin Mary on a wooden table-board, which came from Mary's house in Nazareth and was made by her husband, the carpenter Joseph. Saint Helena, the mother of Constantine the Great, is credited with the discovery around the same time she discovered the Church of Nativity in Bethlehem (*see* page 70) and the Church of Holy Sepulchre (*see* page 68), upon the instructions of her recently converted son (and Roman Emperor). Her discovery of

several Christian sites and artefacts saw her labelled throughout history as the "First Pilgrim of the Holy Land". It is said the painting arrived in Czestochowa in 1384 after Helena passed it on to Constantine. It was bequeathed to Charlemagne in the 8th century, and then finally it went to Jasna Góra after Duke Władysław, ruler of Poland in the 14th century, saw in his dream a vision of the Black Madonna in a wooden church atop a limestone hill – Jasna Góra – where it has remained ever since.

Located above the altar in a central chapel in the monastery complex, this sacred masterpiece is unveiled twice a day (at 6 a.m. and 1.30 p.m.) and is the principal spiritual purpose of most pilgrimages to the site. In the last six centuries, word spread around the world of the miracles ascribed to the Black Madonna, increasing the number of pilgrims who travel to Jasna Góra. In 1430, the Hussites (who denounced devotion to the Blessed Mother) attacked the shrine. As one of them slashed the painting – damage visible today – the Hussite collapsed and died. There are multiple similar tales of the painting's protective power worthy of further research, but the Black Madonna's true beauty has to be seen with your own eyes to be believed."

Opposite: Pope Clement XI issued a canonical coronation to the painting of the Black Madonna on 8 September 1717.

Međugorje

VISIONS OF THE VIRGIN MARY ENTRANCE AN ENTIRE COMMUNITY

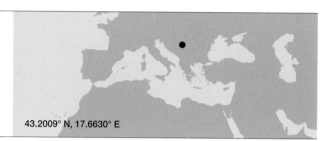

- ✳ Bosnia & Herzegovina
- ✝ Roman Catholic
- ⛉ 1981

- 👥 1 million
- 🗓 May–September
- ⛰ 0.2 hectares (.07 acres)

43.2009° N, 17.6630° E

A spiritual site steeped in mysticism and miracles, Međugorje is a hugely popular pilgrimage destination, as well as a living monument to the deep roots of the Catholic faith in Bosnia & Herzegovina.

On 24 June 1981, this small parish, situated on Herzegovina's Mount Podbrdo (*Međugorje* means "between mountains") 100 kilometres (62 miles) from the Bosnian capital, Sarajevo, became a spiritual centre point for Catholics and believers all around the world, for one simple reason.

Visions and apparitions are not altogether uncommon in strict Catholic countries – Ireland has many such cases every year – but few of them get past the Church's strict processes to become established and accredited. Sometimes, and this is the case with Međugorje, so many people attended with their own pilgrimages that the Church is forced to take notice. It's a moving story.

Two young girls – Marija Lunetti and Mirjana Soldo – claimed they saw an illuminated figure of a woman holding an infant, high on a hill of Podbrdo. They immediately understood the vision to be the Virgin Mary. The infant was Jesus. The next day, Marija and Mirjana returned to the mountain, as if called by the spirit, and – with the addition of friends Vicka, Ivan, Ivanka and Jakov – witnessed once again the vision of Mary, the Blessed Mother. Mary introduced herself to the children as the "Queen of Peace", and promised to return regularly in order to share with them her Son's secrets and to bring the world back to Jesus. One of these secrets is the promise of the Lasting Sign, a miracle to appear upon Mount Podbrdo, sent directly by God to prove the apparitions are genuine. Until the Lasting Sign appears, Mary regularly manifests herself on the hill through the eyes of her six child visionaries, sending messages of faith at important intervals throughout the year.

Today, Međugorje is a popular pilgrimage destination, with more than one million Catholics visiting every year. To honour the Virgin Mary's request, a "Queen of Peace" statue marks the site of the first apparition.

Mount Podbrdo has been renamed Apparition Hill, and pilgrims from around the world climb up to greet the statue of the Virgin Mary in the hope of basking in her spirit. Many believe they feel her presence as they pray.

Until 2010, the apparitions were ignored by the Catholic Church. However, in May 2019, the Vatican officially authorized pilgrimages to Međugorje, with Pope Francis himself claiming that "People go to Međugorje and convert. People who encounter God, change their lives... this spiritual fact can't be ignored." The first Vatican-sanctioned pilgrimage occurred in August 2019 and more than 60,000 Catholics from 97 countries, including high-ranking Church officials, archbishops and 700 Catholic priests, journeyed to the site at the feet of Queen of Peace statue.

Since 1981, 50 million pilgrims have visited Međugorje, making it Europe's third most visited apparition site in terms of visitors.

Opposite above: The Church of St James the Apostle, close to the site of the original apparition.

Nasir-Al-Mulk Mosque

A TECHNICOLOUR DREAM OF DEVOTION SHINING BRIGHT IN IRAN

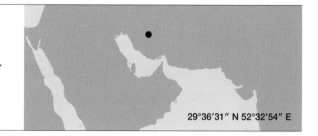

⊕ Iran

✝ Islam

🏛 1876

👤 N/A

📅 March–May; September–October

⊕ 2,980 m² (3,564 sq. yd)

29°36′31″ N 52°32′54″ E

Located in the heart of the legendary Iranian city of Shiraz, the "Pink Mosque" is a technicolour symphony of spirituality for the senses, and was recently voted one of the world's top five most incredible mosques.

Beloved as something so beautiful that upon entering through its resplendent blue, yellow, pink, azure and white porch, visitors feel as if they are immersed in a rainbow reverie, Nasir-Al-Mulk Mosque is indeed a humbling kaleidoscope of colour. With a plethora of pink tiles adorning its large exterior with seemingly endless, beautiful floral tiling that carpets the interior – this sacred, and once private, mosque glows with both physical and spiritual illuminance inside and outside. The experience of visiting here may be dream-like, but its purpose as a centre of worship is very real.

This majestic building was devised and ordered by Mirza Hasan Ali Nasir al-Mulk, a lord of the Qajar dynasty, which ruled over Iran from 1789 to 1925. At the time of construction the Shah was Naser al-Din Shah Qajar. It took only 12 years to construct and was finally completed in 1888. Three architects were involved, predominantly Mohammad Hasan-e-Memār, who was also responsible for the beautiful Eram Garden in Shiraz, as well as Mohammad Rezā Kāshi-Sāz-e-Širāzi and Mohammad Hosseini Shirazi.

The mosque was built right in the centre of Shiraz, the capital of the Fars province, a place that has always been historically identified as Persia and the gateway to Persepolis.

Mosques, like temples and churches, may all follow a more or less similar architectural template, such as having minarets and five concaves, but each has a unique design that is distinct enough for it to stand apart from, or better, its nearby rivals. Nasir al Mulk wanted to leave a lasting legacy and be remembered for his devotion, so he decided to create an unforgettable monument to Allah. He reputedly asked his architects to plan a structure that would be verging on the indescribable. The result is a mosque that goes way above and beyond a simple spiritual calling. Frequently described as a sacred space where light and worship intertwine, the mosque bursts to life with the sunrise when its famous stained-glass (incidentally a Syrian invention) windows and surfaces twinkle and sparkle with the sun's rays. Light floods the entire mosque with vibrant beams that bounce off the ground, walls, arches and its two towers, offering a pure reflection and representation of Allah's divine iridescence. This is a dazzling spiritual encounter that echoes down the years.

Other highlights include the entrance porch, which is decorated with highly coloured Qajar tiles (mainly produced in Tehran, these often intricately detailed tiles became popular in the 19th century and have since become popular and collectible), the wooden entrance door and the notable *shabestans* (underground spaces).

Opposite: Visitors most often arrive for morning prayer before 9.00 a.m. in autumn and winter, and before 11.00 a.m. in spring and summer, to catch a glimpse of the sunrise illumination.

Reims Cathedral

A CELEBRATION OF CHRISTIANITY, CHAMPAGNE AND CORONATIONS

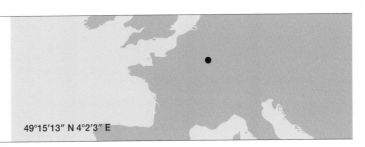

⊛ France

✝ Roman Catholic

🏛 1211

👥 1.5 million

📅 June–September

📍 81 m (266 ft) (height)

49°15′13″ N 4°2′3″ E

Reims Cathedral is the most important Gothic cathedral in France, perhaps even the world. To walk the famed length of its hallowed, historic, haunting hall is a spiritual experience that has stood the test of a thousand years.

More than 60 years in the making – and now more than 1,000 years old – Reims Cathedral's survival is as remarkable as its stunning architecture. Throughout its incredible history, the cathedral has been subject to repeated creation, destruction and restoration. It survived the French Revolution and was torn to rubble by more than 300 large-calibre artillery shells during the First World War, before being restored to its now-pristine condition in 1937.

Reims Cathedral is located in the Champagne region of north-east France, and it is built upon the ruins of a former church, which had been ordered by Constantine the Great, the first Roman Emperor, and the man who brought Christianity to the emerging European nation in the 4th century CE.

And it was Reims Cathedral – not Paris, the capital – that had the distinction of holding the seat of power. It has been the site of coronation for 25 of France's kings, including the first, King Clovis I (466–511 CE), the man who united the Frankish tribes under one ruler. It was also the coronation site for Charles VII, the famous king who bought peace and prosperity to France after the Hundred Years' War. Charles VII was also the crowning achievement of teenager Joan of Arc's ambition. At his coronation at Reims, Joan kneeled before him and exclaimed, "Noble King, now is accomplished the pleasure of God, who willed that I should raise the siege of Orléans and should bring you to this city of Reims to receive your holy coronation, thus showing that you are the true King, him to whom the throne of France must belong."

Dedicated to the Virgin Mary, Reims Cathedral is still a hugely popular tourist and pilgrimage destination, with more than 1.5 million visitors attending every year. Since 1991 it has been a UNESCO World Heritage site, revered for its Outstanding Universal Value. Each year, these many pilgrims bask in the shadows of the two iconic 81-metre (266-ft)-tall towers on its western facade, and its many famous art masterpieces, including the Coronation of the Virgin that stands proudly in the western facade. Once a year it is lit up by a fantastic light show.

It is notably the longest cathedral in Europe, stretching to 149 metres (489 ft), nearly every inch of which is adorned with sculptures, tapestries, gilding, mosaics, stained-glass windows and paintings. In addition, the walls of the cathedral contain more than 2,300 statues – more than any other religious structure in the world. The most famous of these is the *Ange au sourire* (the Smiling Angel), also known as the angel of Reims.

Reims is the world's champagne capital, home to the largest, oldest and greatest champagne houses in the world; newly crowned kings would be toasted with a glass.

Opposite: Reims Cathedral, known as Notre-Dame de Reims ("our lady of Reims"), is famed around the world as one of the best examples of French High Gothic.

Sagrada Família

BARCELONA'S SKY-SCRAPING SALUTE TO THE HOLY SPIRIT AND FAMILY

- ✳ Spain
- ✝ Roman Catholic
- 🏛 1882
- 👥 4.5 million
- 📅 Anytime
- ⬡ 0.4 hectares (1.1 acres)

41°24'13" N 2°10'28" E

One of the most recognized sacred and spiritual sites on earth, Barcelona's Gaudí-designed La Sagrada Família deserves every photon of spotlight shined upon its stunning Gothic and curvilinear Art Nouveau architecture.

No hyperbole can match the majesty of this monumental Spanish masterpiece. And like any true *magnum opus* it has taken ages to (almost) complete. And this basilica, after 150 years, remarkably, still has much more impressing to do. Construction is set to be finished in 2026, nearly 150 years after the first construction was started.

When the building is completed, however, it will be an even more beautiful sight for the world to behold. As of 2022, only eight towers have been built, rising up into the Barcelona skyline. On completion, in total, there will be 18 towers (12 to represent Jesus's apostles; four for Matthew, Mark, Luke and John; one to honour the Virgin Mary). The final, central tower, will be the tallest, and has been designed to reach a staggering 170 metres (558 ft) towards the heavens and will, naturally, symbolize Jesus Christ.

Despite its imposing height, the basilica's Spanish architect, Antoni Gaudí, was adamant his own landmark should be no taller than God's own handiwork, so he designed it to be 1 metre (3 ft) lower than the city's highest point, which is Barcelona's tallest mountain, Montjuïc.

When Gaudí died in 1926, the basilica was one-quarter complete. He dedicated his final years to overseeing its construction, saying, "My good friends are dead; I have no family and no clients, no fortune nor anything. Now I can dedicate myself entirely to the Church", adding, "The church of La Sagrada Família is made by the people and is mirrored in them. It is a work that is in the hands of God and the will of the people." The church was, indeed, made, and paid for, by the people of Barcelona, relying solely on private donations to fund its lengthy construction; this hasn't harmed its progress.

And it is a huge tourist and pilgrimage site; certainly one of the biggest in Spain. During the hot summer months more than 30,000 visitors bask in the structure's magnificence each day. Many will try to time their arrival to be at the 'golden hour', just before sunset in order to see the basilica's stained-glass windows illuminate the numerous mosaics and artworks below, bathing the cathedral in dreamy, heavenly light. Naturally, this was deliberate. "Light achieves maximum harmony at an inclination of 45 degrees, since it resides on objects in a way that is neither horizontal nor vertical", said Gaudí of his masterpiece's main attraction. "It offers the most perfect vision of objects and their most exquisite nuances."

Although famed for his beautiful, nature-inspired organic work that the basilica shows off so well, Antoni Gaudí was not the original architect, that honour going to the now almost-forgotten (on this project) Francisco de Paula del Villar y Lozano. How different this monumental landmark could have been.

Above: The amazingly colourful roof of the basilica. The Sagrada Família was promoted from a cathedral in 2010.

Sheikh Zayed Grand Mosque

ABU DHABI'S ALL-WHITE MARBLE MAJESTY

 UAE   1 million+

 Islam   April/May; Sept–Oct

 1996   12 hectares (30 acres)

24.412° N 54.474° E

Abu Dhabi's largest devotion to Allah is an oasis of modern architectural marvel, a gleaming all-white marble mosque that separates the brilliant blue skies above and the golden desert dunes beneath.

For more than 40,000 daily worshippers, Sheikh Zayed Grand Mosque is the largest in the United Arab Emirates (UAE), and a sacred place of worship for the nation's 75 per cent Muslims. The mosque was the vision of the country's first president, Sheikh Zayed bin Sultan Al Nahyan, the driving force behind the formation of the UAE in 1971, successfully uniting the seven states: Abu Dhabi, Dubai, Sharjah, Ajman, Umm Al Quwain, Ras Al Khaimah and Fujairah. President for 33 years until his death in 2004, Sheikh Zayed was buried in the building he built, and beloved, in honour of his last wishes.

During the entirety of the lengthy construction, Zayed remained true to his vision: the mosque was to be a symbol of the unity he craved for his people. And today, the Grand Mosque is open for everyone to visit, including non-Muslims. It was founded on the fundamental principles of spreading tolerance, peace and co-existence, as well as encouraging prayer for the devout and it continues to follow those principles. The whole edifice, itself a fusion of three local architectural styles (Mughal, Moorish and Ottoman) screams unity loud and proud. More than 3,000 artisans and craftsmen were assembled from around the world, as well as a wealth of natural materials, including marble, stone, ceramics, gold and crystals.

Perhaps the most shining light of the sheikh's vision, and quite probably what has become the most iconic feature of this world-famous mosque, was to use 100,000 tonnes (98,420 tons) of white marble, imported from Macedonia. Sheikh Zayed chose white marble quite deliberately, as a representation of the building's core intentions: peace and purity. The marbled mosque gleams a bright white every night thanks to lunar illumination, making it truly a shining beacon for all to see, even in the dark.

Mirroring – and at times possibly even exceeding – the stunning exterior lies even more lavish opulence inside, evidence that leaves little wonder as to why the total construction bill came out at a reputed USD$500 million, though that amount pales in comparison to the alleged US$75 billion price tag of the Masjid Al-Haram in Mecca, which was known as the most expensive religious structure ever built. Regardless of the cost of this grand mosque, it is truly stunning in every way, its peaceful, corridors smooth, quiet and calm.

Opposite: The main prayer hall features what is apparently the world's largest carpet. It also contains 96 marble pillars, each delicately inlaid with mother-of-pearl.

St Basil's Cathedral

RUSSIA'S MOST RECOGNIZABLE RELIGIOUS ICON

✳ Russia	👥 20 million	
✝ E. Orthodox Christianity	📅 2 August	
🏛 1555	📍 64 m² (689 sq. ft)	

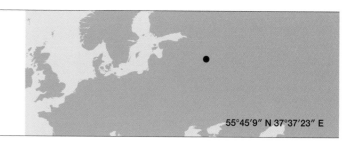

55°45'9" N 37°37'23" E

The superstar attraction at the heart of Moscow's Red Square, Saint Basil's Cathedral, with its famous domes, is a stunning technicoloured cathedral and the cause of celebration as well as controversy for Eastern Orthodox Christianity.

Saint Basil's Cathedral is, by far, the most recognizable landmark in Russia, and its foundation stone was laid in 1555 at the southern-most spot of Red Square in the country's capital city, Moscow. It has been at the centre of many of the Kremlin's decisions and events, historical and political, ever since. It is viewed in the background of political rallies, troop demonstrations and news reports alike; it is synonymous with the Russian state and has been for centuries.

Ordered to be constructed by the first Tsar of Russia, the Grand Prince of Moscow Ivan Vasilyevich, or Ivan the Terrible, as history sees fit to label him. He was given this label for his seeming affection for war and military conflicts, as well as his intense rages. Indeed, Saint Basil's was built in honour of his armies, for their many victories in battle that served to feed his desire for an ever-larger empire. And vengeful, as according to one legend, the cathedral's main architects, Ivan Barma and Postnik Yakovlev, were blinded by Ivan so that they could never surpass its design anywhere else. However, evidence of their subsequent work elsewhere in Russia indicates this is myth.

Dedicated to the Virgin Mary, Saint Basil's remains a grand spiritual icon for Russian disciples of Christ, and a pilgrimage for millions, despite the structure's status as more of a secular tourist attraction than a place of worship. Each year 20 million people visited the cathedral until 2022 at least, a number that made it one of the most visited tourist locations on earth.

For Eastern Orthodox Christians, Saint Basil's Cathedral represents Jerusalem, the Heavenly City. Famed for being nine chapels in one, and represented by nine colourful onion domes – the tallest being 47.5 metres (156 ft) – four of which are aligned with particular points on the compass to designate their alleged position between heaven and earth. The domes of the Russian Orthodox cathedral have not always been so colourful, however. Originally the entire structure was white, with only the domes shining gold. In the mid-17th century, the cathedral was painted in multiple colours in order to look more visually impactful against Russia's nearly-all-year-round overcast skies.

The ninth chapel to be added to the cathedral commemorates Basil Vasily, or Basil the Blessed, the saint behind the name. Basil was well known in the city as Moscow's "holy fool", an eccentric and homeless prophet, a future-teller and early Robin Hood-a-like who shamed the rich to give to the poor. It was Basil who predicted a fire in 1547 that engulfed the city and destroyed one-third of all buildings. At Basil's funeral, Ivan the Terrible himself acted as pall-bearer. Basil was canonized in 1588, and the cathedral named in his honour, finally giving Saint Basil a home of his own.

Opposite: In 1990, the Kremlin, Red Square and the cathedral became a UNESCO World Heritage Site, one of 16 UNESCO cultural sites in Russia.

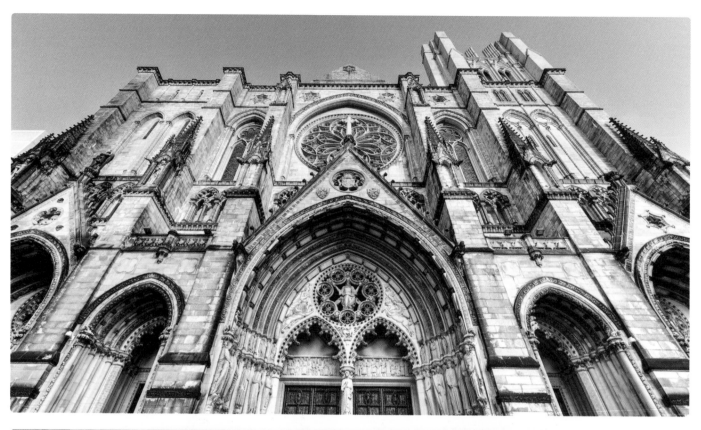

St John the Divine

SACRED SPACE IN THE CENTRE OF NEW YORK CITY

⊛ USA

✝ Christian

🏛 1892

👥 500,000

📅 27 December (St John's Feast Day)

⊛ 1.12 hectares (2.7 acres)

40°48'13" N 73°57'41" W

People in New York City may look up to the stunning skyscrapers, but it is the mother church of America's devotion to Christ, St John the Divine, that reaches highest into the souls of the city's spirituality.

If you find yourself looking for some spiritual respite among New York's bustling metropolis, chances are before long you'll end up at 1047 Amsterdam Avenue, between West 110th Street and West 113th Street, in Morningside Heights. This is a neighbourhood, where, for more than 130 years, St John the Divine has stood tall and served the community for prayer and worship for the city's 60 per cent Christian population, as well as hundreds of thousands of secular visitors seeking illumination in its blessed architecture.

The foundation stone to this breathtaking Romanesque, Byzantine and Gothic-inspired building was laid on the birthday of Saint John the Divine, 27 December 1892. In order to decide which direction to face the altar – the holiest part of any Christian structure, and traditionally found in the eastern side closest to the rising sun, a symbol of resurrection – Bishop Potter, the church's founding father, stood in the centre of the 5-hectare (12-acre)-site at sunrise and looked to see where the sun rose. In this way, the site of St John the Divine is in keeping with several construction traditions for religious buildings: it is erected on high ground (Morningside Heights is at the highest natural elevation in the whole city) and it is designed in a cruciform shape – a Roman cross.

Ensconced within the construction of the building are several other features that point to the structure's sanctity. The number seven, the most prominent symbol in the book of Revelation, the

final book of the New Testament and the Bible, and believed to have been written by John, the Divine Evangelist Apostle, can be seen around the site as a way to signpost the seven miracles of Christ, especially in the seven chapels and seven lamps illuminating the high altar.

The church's namesake, Saint John the Evangelist, was one of the 12 original apostles of Jesus, and the disciple that Jesus perhaps loved the most, according to scripture. John's account in his gospel, his Three Letters of John, and the book of Revelation, highlight that John was a close friend of Jesus and most trusted to carry on his teachings. As he did.

In what could be considered as a grand metaphor for the never-ending spiritual growth that all religious devotees seek throughout their lives, the Cathedral of Saint John the Divine remains an incomplete masterpiece. *A Guide to the Cathedral* reported in 1921 that, due to the original Gothic building methods intended to complete the construction, it would take 700 years for the cathedral to be finished – some time in 2592. As such, the cathedral, affectionately, has been nicknamed "St John the Unfinished". Regardless, St John the Divine remains the largest cathedral in the world and the fifth largest church.

Opposite: The first service was held in January 1899, with much of the cathedral still under construction.

St Mark's Basilica

OTHERWORLDLY OASIS IN A WORLD-FAMOUS LAGOON CITY

- ✦ Italy
- ✝ Roman Catholic
- 🏛 828 CE
- 👥 20 million
- 📅 25 April (Feast of St Mark)
- 📍 0.5 hectares (1.2 acres)

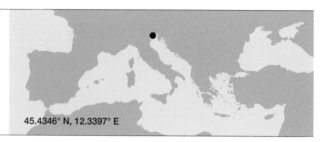

45.4346° N, 12.3397° E

So much more than one of the world's most romantic holiday destinations, the Italian city of Venice holds a tapestry of treasures all around its 170 famous canals and seemingly countless places of worship. Shrouded in spiritual and scenic splendour, at its centre is the postcard-perfect Piazza San Marco and the blessed St Mark's Basilica.

In a city dominated by historic – and iconic – canals, churches, gondolas and rialtos, Piazza San Marco still stands out as Venice's most popular tourist attraction. The focal point of this Venetian obsession, however, is St Mark's Basilica, which serves as the light at the end of the path for the millions of Roman Catholic pilgrims who arrive in the lagoon city to pay their respects to Mark the Evangelist. The basilica also marks the spot for history lovers, romantics, artists and tourists, all of whom have a desire to experience first-hand one of the most significant, and sacred, churches in all of Christendom, known for its history and eye-catching beauty.

It was founded in 832 CE to house the remains of Saint Mark – one of the four Apostles, along with Matthew, Luke and John, who was the author attributed with the creation of the four Gospel accounts in the New Testament. According to the legend, in 828 CE, Venetian priests Buono da Malamocco and Rustico da Torcello smuggled Saint Mark's body back to Venice in barrels, after bribing priests in Alexandria, Egypt, to part with the relics. Ever since, the basilica has grown in size and sanctity as a testament to Saint Mark.

The resting place is now home to a number of priceless religious relics and treasures from all over the world, which are installed in the vaults and the hallowed halls – including the irreplaceable Horses of Saint Mark (the Triumphal Quadriga or Horses of the Hippodrome of Constantinople), and the universally recognized Pala d'Oro, a Byzantine altar screen of gold, studded with thousands of pearls, emeralds and other gems.

There are also more than 8,000 square metres (85,000 sq. ft) of gold mosaics under the basilica's famous domes and bell tower. If visitors enter the basilica at different times of day, the depicted scenes and colours of the mosaics are illuminated by sunlight differently, showing off the ingenuity of the structure's architecture even further.

At the entrance of the basilica stands the 98-metre (323-ft)-high iconic bell tower, which was originally constructed in the 9th century, but rebuilt in 1903 following its collapse. Today, the bell tower is a beacon for Catholic pilgrims, announcing the end of their particular spiritual journey.

In a city that can be bustling and overcrowded at times, St Mark's Basilica continues to deliver as a beautiful, spiritual oasis of calm and beauty.

Opposite and left: The front of the basilica, which was carefully decorated in the 14th and 15th centuries by a number of well-known Tuscan artists. Inside the building are a number of beautiful artworks, murals and paintings, including a decoration designed by Titian in the 16th century.

St Peter's Basilica

CHRISTENDOM'S SPIRITUAL CENTRE AND SITE OF THE SPECIAL SAINT'S CRUCIFIXION

✳ Vatican City

✝ Roman Catholic

🏛 1506

👥 1 million

📅 29 June (Feast of St Peter)

🗺 2 hectares (5 acres)

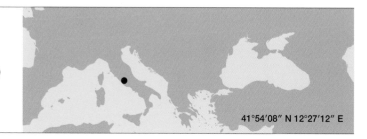

41°54'08" N 12°27'12" E

At the crux of the smallest country in the world – Vatican City – lies the largest church in all of Christendom, and the centre of the Catholic religion: St Peter's Basilica. More than a million people visit annually, to see the Pope or simply take in the majesty of this impressive place.

Since the death of Saint Peter in 64 CE, the spiritual home-from-home for 1.5 billion Catholics and the seat of Roman Catholic power has stood the test of time. St Peter's Basilica, the burial location of the leader of the 12 Apostles of Christ, is built upon the ruins of the old tomb where it is said Peter was crucified upside-down. That was demolished in 1505, and it had previously stood for a stunning 12 centuries.

The basilica today is considered the holiest landmark in all of contemporary Christendom. It's little wonder that it welcomes more than 55,000 visitors each and every day to gaze upon its incredible Renaissance architecture and wander through the hallowed halls that are 72 metres (236 ft) in length, and 49 metres (160 ft) wide. It is a space that covers an area of 2 hectares (5 acres). Equally famous, and large, is the Basilica's entrance: the huge open space of St Peter's Square. Every year, on the Feast of Saint Peter, 29 June, the square welcomes the prayers of 300,000 pilgrims. The Pope presides over regular blessings and Catholic pilgrims to the site can catch site of him and attend a mass; of course, all are welcome.

In 1505, Pope Julius II launched a competition to find an architect worthy of a design he wanted for the "grandest building in Christendom." Italian architect Donato Bramante won the commission, with his floor plan in the shape of a large cross which was covered by a large dome – the architectural inspiration for many more of the world's churches. Bramante died in 1514, leaving another famed architect, Michelangelo, in 1546, to be appointed chief architect, aged 71. The basilica was finally completed on 18 November, 1626, some 120 years after the foundation stone was laid on the sacred site.

One of the several masterpieces housed inside the basilica is a Michelangelo sculpture, the *Pietà*, depicting the Virgin Mary cradling the dead body of Jesus after his body was removed from the cross.

At the time of construction, St Peter's Basilica was the grandest and most ambitious spiritual structure ever. It was also the most expensive, allegedly costing 50 million ducats (gold coins), approximately the equivalent of £4 billion today. The basilica's size matches its spiritual sacredness, however. The dome, painted by Michelangelo, is the largest in the world, reaching 136 metres (446ft) tall and 136 metres (446 ft) wide.

"And I say to thee: That thou art Peter; and upon this rock I will build my church, and the gates of hell shall not prevail against it", so said Jesus Christ to Peter, as told in the Gospel of Matthew. And, with his body as the sacrifice, Peter did exactly that.

Opposite and overleaf: The basilica will forever remain as the tallest building in Rome, with no structures permitted to be built any taller.

St Sophia Cathedral

FRESCOES AND UNESCO UNITE FOR UKRAINE'S OLDEST SACRED SITE

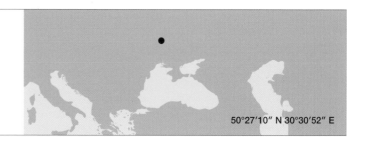

- ✳ Ukraine
- ✝ Orthodox Christianity
- 🏛 1011
- 👥 1 million
- 🗓 May–August
- 🗺 721 m² (7,760 sq. ft)

50°27′10″ N 30°30′52″ E

Situated in the historic centre of the country's capital, Kyiv, St Sophia Cathedral was the first world heritage site in Ukraine. It shares its spiritual specialness, and UNESCO inscription, with nearby Pechersk Lavra, a majestic labyrinth of monastic caves.

In 1037, Duke Yaroslav the Wise of Kyiv founded the Saint Sophia Cathedral in honour of Hagia Sophia (*see* page 78) in Istanbul, which was dedicated to the Holy Wisdom, rather than the 6th-century Saint Sophia. Today, the cathedral, which casts its shadow over Ukraine's capital city and peers down on the meandering Dnipro river, stands tall as a symbolic representation of the age when Kyiv was the capital of the far-reaching Kyivan Rus' Empire. The inhabitants of this great realm were the rulers of the Ukraine-Russian borders from the 9th to the 13th centuries. The site and the building itself also show the unification of cultural interaction between the Kyivan Rus', the Byzantine Empire and Western Europe. As UNESCO wrote of the Cathedral in 1996, the year it was inscribed, it "represents a masterpiece of human creative genius in both its architectural conception and its remarkable decoration."

The interior decoration of the cathedral is, indeed, a work of genius. Lining the halls and walls of the domes are 3,000 square metres (32,291 sq. ft) of frescoes that are of enormous spiritual significance, as well as being quite beautiful. The vaults beneath, and the golden-green domes occupy 260 square metres (2,798 sq. ft) of mosaics depicting the most significant scenes of Orthodox Christian tradition.

Located in another part of the city, underground, is the Kyiv-Pechersk Lavra Monastery, where the relics of saints lie buried in caves. Both sites are owned by the state. Both St Sophia and the caves are Ukraine's most important Christian pilgrimage offers to the world, with more than one million pilgrims visiting each year. The cave complex is a labyrinth of catacombs, full of mummified monks, religious relics and icons.

Certainly justifying their official label as one of the 'Seven Wonders of Ukraine', the cathedral and grounds are beautiful to visit, a haven of peace and calm in a busy, bustling city. The cathedral has had a somewhat checkered history, with various regimes designating it to be in the care of the state, rather than organized religious orders. Ukraine, as part of the USSR, had a traditionally anti-religious rulership, and the cathedral was due to be demolished in the 1930s. It was saved from this fate, however, unlike the neighbouring St Michael's monastery, which was destroyed around 1935. (It was subsequently rebuilt and repopulated with many original artifacts that had been removed prior to its destruction.)

The cathedral complex includes a number of other impressive buildings, comprising the Metropolitan's Residence (currently used as an exhibition/conference hall), the bell tower, the refectory church, a high school, a library and consistory. Entry is best through the impressive Zaborowski Gate.

Opposite: Built over nine centuries, the cathedral is now a fundamental part of the Kyiv skyline and a national monument.

CHAPTER 3

Pilgrimages

Some religions require daily acts of faith, some weekly. Others require a single, major act of pilgrimage to show devotion. Nearly all religions offer a journey or trial that rewards the loyal member. This chapter showcases some of the most significant, lengthy rituals that continue to be practised, some for thousands of years.

Batu Caves

THE SACRED ROCK-CUT CAVE TEMPLE WHERE GOLDEN LORD MURUGAN STANDS GUARD

(✷) Malaysia

(†) Hinduism

(▥) 1860

(👤) 1 million

(▦) December–April

(◉) 42.7 m (140 ft) (statue height)

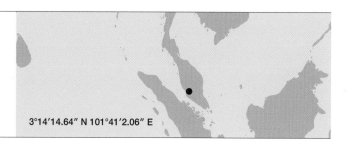

3°14′14.64″ N 101°41′2.06″ E

Enshrined as a sacred Hindu site in 1860, the Batu Caves themselves are in fact a lot older – around 400 million years. This cave temple complex is protected by the Hindu god of war – Lord Murugan. It is the tallest statue in Malaysia and the third tallest statue of a Hindu deity in the world.

At the foot of the world-famous 272 breathtaking steps, stands a striking, stunning, giant gold-painted statue of Lord Murugan, 42.7 metres (140 ft) in height. Lord Murugan, the Hindu god of war, is celebrated by Malaysia's Tamil Hindus, who make up roughly 6 per cent of the total Malaysian population. More than 350 tonnes (344 tons) of steel bars, 300 litres (79 gallons) of gold paint, and 1,550 cubic metres (54,738 cu. ft) of concrete was required to be transported up to the caves for construction. Outside of Malaysia, Lord Murugan is more commonly celebrated as Kartikeya. He is the son of creator-god Shiva, and the Parvati, the goddess of fertility, strength and power, and the younger brother of Ganesha. As written in Buddhist and sacred Hindu texts, Murugan is an earthly representation of Shiva's light and wisdom and the vanquisher of all evil. Those that pray to him will overcome their fears.

The Batu Caves is the most popular Hindu shrine outside India, with more than 1 million pilgrims attending over the Thaipusam, which is the Tamil Hindu festival devoted to Murugan. It is held here every year in order to receive the god's grace and destroy their sins. The festival commemorates the occasion when Parvati gave a divine spear to her son, Lord Murugan, to defeat a fiendish demon. For the Hindu community in Malaysia, Thaipusam is the most important religious festival of the year and was first celebrated on this site in 1892. It is now a major

event that attracts pilgrims from all over the world annually. During the festival, followers of Lord Murugan are required to fast in advance for a month as well shave their heads. They are then required to perform what is called the *kavadi attam* dance. Afterwards, a special offering to Lord Murugan should be made. The pilgrimage is an exciting one to behold, with long, snaking lines of people queuing to make their way into the cave complex, make their blessings and then make their way out again.

Used as a series of cave temple and shelters for centuries by the indigenous Temuan people, Batu is just 13 kilometres (8 miles) north Malaysia's huge, sprawling capital, Kuala Lumpur. Its proximity to the capital ensures it becomes a tourist hotspot in the summer months, with visitors keen to see the largest and most popular cave of the three main caverns, the Cathedral Cave, which is 100 metres (300 ft) high. Inside the candlelit cave stand scores of Hindu shrines and inscriptions of Hindu creation tales and legends being brought to life. It all adds up to a feast for multiple senses and an intense spiritual experience, from the cheeky monkeys at the base to the cool caves above.

Opposite: In the Malay language, *Batu* means "rock" and the caves are home to hundreds of thousands of pilgrims at key times of year in the Hindu celebration calender.

Glastonbury

THE RESTING PLACE OF SOME OF THE WORLD'S GREATEST LEGENDS

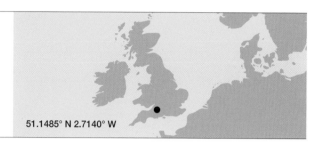

⊛ England

✝ Druid/Christian

🏛 712 CE

👥 500,000

📅 Summer Solstice (21 June)

⚲ 158 m (518 ft) (height)

51.1485° N 2.7140° W

A town rich in ancient legend, energy-laden ley lines, mysticism and – during the iconic music festival on nearby Worthy Farm – mud. There is nowhere else on earth like Glastonbury, with its unique mixture of ancient history and modern music.

Glastonbury is often called the spiritual home of England, and it certainly merits the label. Nestled snugly in the rolling green fields of the aptly-named Somerset (*Sumersaeta* – "Land of the Summer People"), Glastonbury is the resting place of envy-inducing religious relics as well as a few of the most spiritually significant sightseeing in the country. For centuries, religious pilgrims, new age travellers and tourists alike have assembled in Glastonbury for its choice selection of spiritual sites, which include Glastonbury's Old Church, known by some as the first Christian church in the British Isles.

At the centre of all the fuss, primarily, lies Glastonbury Tor, itself the ancient ruins of a church, situated atop its own perfectly conical, all-natural hill. Today, only the tower survives – and it can be seen for miles around, often shrouded in a mystic curtain of cloud cover, a towering beacon of Somerset's spirituality. One thousand years ago the hill was an island, surrounded by a large lake. In Celtic folklore, the hill and the lake are the magical Isle of Avalon, final resting place of King Arthur.

Down below the Tor, in the parish of Glastonbury, lies the ruins of the legendary Glastonbury Abbey, a monastery built in 712 CE. Today, legend tells us that King Arthur, the famed 5th-century ruler and his equally famous wife, Queen Guinevere, were buried in the grounds of the now ruined abbey. It is believed that monks unearthed Arthur's tomb, digging up his very own bones and a scrap of hair, alongside a lead cross that

was inscribed with the now-famous words, "Here lies buried the renowned King Arthur in the Isle of Avalon".

According to certain stories, King Arthur came to Glastonbury in search of the Holy Grail. That was Jesus Christ's chalice at the Last Supper and the cup containing the spilled blood of Christ himself, as caught by Joseph of Arimathea, in the aftermath of Jesus's crucifixion. Joseph of Arimathea, it is said, travelled to Britain with the Holy Grail to Glastonbury, where he buried it below what is now Glastonbury Tor. Eternal life is promised to those who drink from the cup. Arthur never managed to find the Grail, though his knight, Galahad the pure of heart, did. The whereabouts of the Grail is now unknown.

Skip forward a few years, to 1970, and Michael Eavis, a resident of the former Isle of Avalon himself, organized the first ever Glastonbury Festival at his nearby farm in Pilton, attracting thousands of spiritual pilgrims seeking their own Holy Grail. Today, it is the largest, and greatest, music and contemporary arts event in the world, attracting more than 200,000 revellers, new (and old) age spiritualists and legendary musicians every year. The town of Glastonbury could not be a more suitable spiritual home for such fun.

Opposite: The name Glastonbury is a corruption of the Saxon word *Glæstyngabyrig*. For tourists in search of a spiritual fix, the town is also renowned as a vortex of energy created by the crossing of two ley lines.

Kaaba

A HOUSE OF GOD AT THE HEART OF THE HOLIEST OF ISLAMIC CITIES

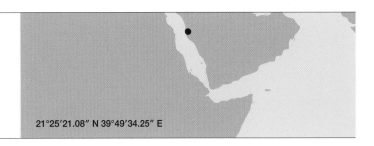

⊛ Saudi Arabia

✝ Islam

🏛 608 CE

👥 20 million

📅 Hajj

⛰ 13.1 m (43 ft) (height)

21°25'21.08" N 39°49'34.25" E

For Muslims, this is a vastly important spiritual destination. At the centre of the worldwide Islamic faith is its cube-shaped heart: Kaaba, Islam's first sacred shrine. It is located within Masjid al-Haram, the Great Mosque, the final stop of the Hajj pilgrimage. And that is in the centre of the holiest of all Islamic cities – Mecca.

Every Muslim is expected to make a pilgrimage to Mecca, and specifically to the Kaaba, at least once in their lifetime. This pilgrimage to Mecca is known as a Hajj and occurs in the final month of the Islamic lunar calendar. The gathering is considered the world's largest human meeting, with more than 2.9 million Muslims coming together at the Great Mosque. (An additional 6.5 million pilgrims arrive annually for the Umrah pilgrimage, which can take place at any time throughout the year.) When pilgrims arrive, they must circumambulate the Kaaba seven times, a practice known as *tawaf*. This moving circle of Muslims symbolizes the constancy and eternity of Allah, with each revolution around the cube representing a stage in the seven layers of sky and the seven souls of man and a sense of allegiance and unity to the creator; it is deeply symbolic.

While the Kaaba is a beacon of light to billions, it is, of course, shrouded in darkness, not least by its own *kiswah*, the cloth that covers it. The cube's history alone has more than enough mystery to fill 1,000 pages. It has been destroyed, damaged, rebuilt and renovated several times in the last 1,000 years. The black stone – which is a rock that is set into the eastern corner of the Kaaba – is the most spiritually important part of the cube, and it was once stolen and held for ransom for 20 years. It was subsequently returned to its holy resting place.

According to Muslim legend, the black stone fell from heaven (it is dark in colour, like a meteorite) and Adam and Eve were drawn to it after God cast them out of the Garden of Eden. Eve landed in Jeddah in Saudi Arabia and Adam in Sri Lanka (at Adam's Peak – *see* page 128), but after themselves making a pilgrimage to Mecca, Adam and Eve established the sanctuary there as a substitute for the Garden of Eden on earth. "The black stone came down from paradise and it was whiter than milk, but the sins of the sons of Adam turned it black", said Muhammad.

The Black Stone of Kaaba is said be the only surviving original element of the Kaaba, which, according to Islamic tradition, was a simple rectangular hut built by Abraham and his son, Ismail, as guided by God. This was some 5,000 years before the Prophet Muhammad built a shrine to Adam – making it the first house of worship of all humankind on earth and of great historical interest as well as spiritual significance.

This place of enormous spiritual significance must surely rate as one of the wonders of the contemporary world.

Opposite: Masjid al-Haram, together with Al-Masjid an-Nabawi, the great Mosque in Medina (see page 66), are known as al-Haramain, or "the two Sanctuaries". They are the twin holy cities of Islam and are linked by their incredible spiritual bond.

Lourdes

MODERN, MIRACULOUS HEALING SITE FOR CHRISTIAN PILGRIMS

⊛ France

✝ Christian

🏛 1858

👥 5 million

📅 **15 August,** the Marian Feast of Assumption

🗺 51 hectares (126 acres)

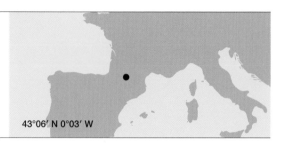

43°06′ N 0°03′ W

Lourdes has remained the most important, and most popular, Christian pilgrimage shrine in the world for more than 150 years. All thanks to a 14-year-old peasant girl, Bernadette Soubirous.

For centuries there have been hundreds of apparitions of the Virgin Mary in various places in the world. Many have elevated the locations into cultural, spiritual and religious sites of tourism and pilgrimage, some of them in most dramatic fashion. In the last two centuries there have been many important "Marian apparitions", as they are known, in Europe. In La Salette, France in 1846; Pontmain, France in 1871; Knock, Ireland in 1879; Castelpetroso, Italy in 1888; Fátima, Portugal in 1916–1917; Garabandal, Spain in 1961; Zeitoun, Egypt in 1968; and Međugorje, Bosnia & Herzegovina in 1981 (*see* page 82). However, as spectral, supernatural sightings go, Bernadette's sighting in Lourdes quite possibly remains the most enduring with religious pilgrims, and the most famous worldwide.

Before 1858, Lourdes, which is located in the foothills of the famous Pyrenees mountains, was like many rural French towns – quiet, modest and untouched by controversy or spectacle. Then, on the evening of 11 February 1858, everything changed.

Teenager Bernadette Soubirous was fetching firewood with her sister near the remote Massabielle Grotto when, suddenly, "a dazzling light and a white figure" of a woman appeared. This female spectre later identified herself as the Virgin Mary. For the next six months, Bernadette returned frequently to the grotto and witnessed sightings of Mary a further 18 times, the teenager each time being seen to enter a trance-like state. It was, indeed, Mary who encouraged Bernadette to build a chapel

at the grotto to honour her earthly presence and her divine son. She also encouraged her to dig a hole in the ground until a small puddle of water appeared, and to drink from that puddle. In due course the puddle became a pool, and now it is the Sacred Spring – and the central attraction that now makes the pretty city of Lourdes so divine.

These days, pilgrims to France drink from and bathe in the spring, believing it has healing properties, and many curing miracles are reported to have taken place at the site over the years. Within 12 months of Bernadette's visions, thousands of pilgrims began to arrive in Lourdes in the hope that they too would see the presence of Mary's spirit. By 1864, the now-famous statue Our Lady of Lourdes was erected to celebrate the apparitions. Today, five million pilgrims from around the world visit the shrine each year, with an estimated 250 million pilgrims of all denominations having visited Lourdes since 1860.

Pope John Paul II visited in 1983 and 2004. "Holy Mary, Mother of believers, Our Lady of Lourdes, pray for us," he said in 2004. As for Bernadette, the other Lady of Lourdes. She was canonized in 1933, becoming Saint Bernadette of Lourdes.

Opposite: Reconstructions of the Lourdes Grotto and the shrine to Virgin Mary now appear all over the world, based on the Massabielle Grotto in Lourdes.

Sanctuary of Fátima

WORSHIP THE MIRACLE OF THE SUN WITH THE VIRGIN MARY

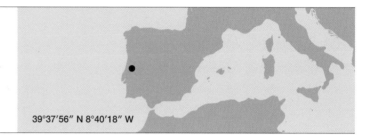

- ✳ Portugal
- ✝ Roman Catholic
- 🏛 1917
- 👥 5 million
- 📅 13 May, 13 October
- 📍 20 hectares (50 acres)

39°37'56" N 8°40'18" W

Across the world, Marian apparitions are the cause of concentrated celebration and sometimes controversy. Today, the Sanctuary of Fátima is the biggest pilgrimage site in Portugal, and the fourth biggest Catholic pilgrimage site in the world.

In the civil parish of Fátima, Ourém, in the heart of Portugal, now stands an awe-inspiring collection of monuments that commemorate two particular days in May 1917, when ten-year-old Lúcia dos Santos and her cousins, Jacinta and Francisco Marto (aged seven and nine respectively) reported to their parents that they had been visited by an apparition of the Virgin Mary.

On their way home from tending a flock of sheep, Lúcia, Francisco and Jacinta witnessed a flash of lightning strike the land. They turned around to see, feel and receive the spirit of Mary. The apparition that was before them told the children that she would return to that same spot in precisely six months' time, before vanishing.

Lúcia ran home and told her parents. They, in turn, told a few more people, and they, in turn, told more. On the appointed date of 13 October, a huge crowd containing around 50,000 Catholic pilgrims had descended on Fátima. All were yearning to repeat what had happened to the three children and witness Mary's return. And Mary did, indeed, return. But her apparition was – to the disappointment of many – only visible in the eyes of the three children who had seen her the first time around.

The crowd stood, amazed, as Lúcia received the vision, and she described it in detail. As the figure appeared, she identified herself as "the Lady of the Rosary" and urged all those present to repent. She further requested that they build a chapel on the spot where she stood. And before she disappeared for a second time, Lúcia told the crowd that the vision of Mary lifted her hands to the sky and exclaimed, "The sun!" The crowd looked up and a "sun miracle" took place – an event that lasted approximately ten minutes. Not all people present saw exactly the same thing, with some reporting they saw the sun dance around in the heavens, while others claimed to see a rainbow of colours spin vibrantly behind the sun. Many thousands of those present saw nothing at all.

The Sanctuary of Fátima is today a gleaming white collection of now-iconic Catholic landmarks, which includes the enormous Basilica of Our Lady of the Rosary, the fourth-largest Catholic church in the world, with a capacity of 8,633, and also the final resting place of Lúcia and her two cousins. There is also shrine which marks the precise spot where the three "little shepherds" saw the original lightning. And finally, the Chapel of the Apparitions was built in 1919 at the request of Mary. It commemorates the exact place where the children saw the spirit of Mary. This spot is a highly symbolic place for the pilgrims to Fátima, and the site of celebrations that take place annually on 13 May and 13 October.

Opposite: Since 1917, every pope has made a pilgrimage to Fátima on 13 May and 13 October to mark the occasion of Mary's earthly visit. He takes mass in Our Lady of the Rosary Basilica.

Santiago de Compostela

SCALLOP SHELLS MARK THE WAY ON THE PATH OF SAINT JAMES

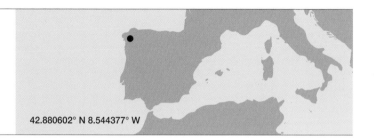

⊛ Spain

✝ Roman Catholic

🏛 1075

👤 300,000

📅 25 July

📍 740 km (460 miles)

42.880602° N 8.544377° W

For 1,000 years, Catholic pilgrims, and those looking for a spiritual path, penance or simply seeking a nice, long walk, have travelled the sacred Camino de Santiago to end up at a most magnificent meeting point – the shrine of Saint James the Great.

James, of course, was better known as one of Jesus Christ's three closest apostles (along with Saint John his brother, and Saint Peter) and the first of the disciples to be martyred. The Cathedral of Santiago de Compostela, the conclusion of the Camino de Santiago (meaning, literally, the Way of Saint James), could not be a more fitting resting place for the great man's remains. Pope Alexander VI agreed in the 15th century, and officially declared the road to be one of the three great pilgrimages of Christendom – equal with Jerusalem and Rome. And in 1987 the Camino de Santiago, which encompasses several routes from Spain, France and Portugal, was declared the first Cultural Route of the Council of Europe.

It was around 820 CE that the first pilgrimage on the Camino de Santiago was carried out, by Alfonso II, King of Asturias. He decided to make the pilgrimage following the discovery of the relics of James. For centuries, famous pilgrimages became a symbol of the struggle of Spanish Christians against Islam. Destroyed by Muslims at the end of the 10th century, the cathedral was completely rebuilt in the following century, and is now well known as an international beacon of Catholic spirituality.

Along the road – or *camino* as the locals call it – to Santiago are scallop shells and yellow arrows that mark the way for pilgrims. Those walking the route also attach shells to their person, so they can be identified as pilgrims. It is a symbol that has been worn since the medieval period.

Traditionally, pilgrims would start their camino from their own home, but these days pilgrims have to walk at least 100 kilometres (62 miles) along the route in order to receive a certificate of completion. There are checkpoints along the way. However, the most famous camino route is the Camino Francés or "French Route" that starts in St-Jean-Pied-de-Port in the foothills of the French Pyrenees. That way is 800 kilometres (500 miles) long and takes the average pilgrim (if there could be such a thing) approximately five weeks to complete, but you can start your camino at any point along the route.

In 2010, Pope Benedict XVI spoke of the renewed importance of the spiritual purpose of the Camino de Santiago in the 21st century. It is estimated that there are now more than 300,000 pilgrims each year, and numbers have been seen to increase a significant amount annually (at least until the Covid-19 pandemic). The pope said, "It is a way sown with so many demonstrations of fervour, repentance, hospitality, art and culture which speak to us eloquently of the spiritual roots of the Old Continent." It is also a beautiful, interesting and deeply spiritual walk.

Opposite: In 1985, the old town area of Santiago de Compostela was designated a UNESCO World Heritage Site, thanks to its Gothic and Baroque architecture, the magnificent Portico of Glory, and the cathedral itself.

Seven Saints of Marrakesh

THE SPIRITUAL SEPULCHRES HOLDING SEVEN SLEEPING SAINTS

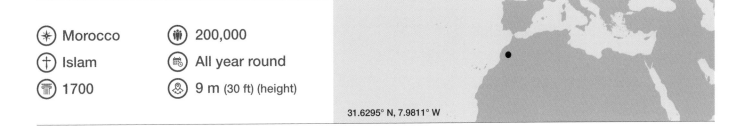

✦ Morocco
✝ Islam
🏛 1700

👥 200,000
🗓 All year round
📍 9 m (30 ft) (height)

31.6295° N, 7.9811° W

Away from the bustle of Marrakesh's world-famous bazaars, resides the Red City's source of spiritual strength. To many Moroccan Muslims, Marrakesh is revered as the "City of the Seven Saints" and these seven monuments pay homage to those great men and their earthly achievements.

For 400 years, the most revered Muslim figures in Moroccan history have been sleeping: they're not dead, according to local legend, but are just waiting to wake up and do more good deeds, in more than 200 tombs located around the walls of the city. The sites of these tombs have been the destinations of the *zaira* pilgrimage since their construction in the 17th century. Ever since, many of the nation's 38 million Muslims (99 per cent of the population) have come here on a pilgrimage – an undertaking of importance. This is similar to the Hajj pilgrimage to the holy city of Mecca in Saudi Arabia, which every adult Muslim should make at least once in their lifetime in order to achieve their own inner spiritual purity.

The *zaira* takes a week to complete, starting traditionally on a Tuesday. Pilgrims commence their trek in the southeast of the city and finish it in the southwest, making a pattern that represents the counter-clockwise walking ritual around the Kaaba – the cube – the centrepiece of Mecca. Each day pilgrims pray at a different tomb before moving on to the next. The Seven Saints legend is based on the "Seven Sleepers of Ephesus" myth, a story of medieval origin that dates back as far as 250 CE, concerning seven local young men who hid inside a cave outside the city of Ephesus (in modern-day Turkey) in order to escape persecution by Romans and Christians. The young men emerged from the cave 300 years later, looking as young as when they went in.

Each of the seven tombs belong to one of the *awliya* (plural of *wali*), great men whom Allah blessed for their high level of devotion to Islam. They were men who taught and studied the teachings of Islam, and today they continue to do so beyond the grave through these monuments. It is believed they were once Christians who converted to Islam after visiting Mecca and meeting Muhammad, and they were venerated for their works after their passing. The names of these saints are: Sidi Youssef Ben Ali, Sidi Qadi Ayyad, Sidi Bel Abbas, Sidi Suleiman Al Jazuli, Sidi Abdel Aziz, Sidi Abdullah Ghazouani and Sidi al-Suhayli.

With Marrakesh home to more than 200 graves of the *awliya*, the ruler Moulay Ismail – second sultan of Morocco (1672–1727) – established the pilgrimage route to the Seven Saints tombs in the 17th century to improve the city's spiritual reputation. This continued in 2005, when the mayor of Marrakesh inaugurated the Place des Septs Saints monument outside Bab Doukkala, near the northeastern gate of the old city, which commemorates the seven in one convenient spot – you'll still have to visit each individual tomb to complete the pilgrimage though.

Opposite: During the pilgrimage, Moroccan Muslims pray to Allah and Muhammad, in the hope of having their wishes fulfilled, to heal their sick and ask for tranquillity within their souls.

Shikoku

JAPAN'S HOOPED AND HEALING HENRO IN HONOUR OF KŌBŌ DAISHI

✳ Japan

✝ Shingon Buddhist

𐄷 Circa 800 CE

👥 100,000

📅 July–September

⛰ 18,900 km² (7,300 sq. mi.)

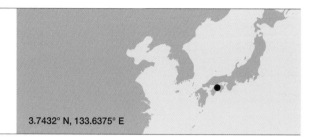

3.7432° N, 133.6375° E

One thousand two hundred years old, one thousand two hundred kilometres (745 miles) long. The Henro, or "88 Temple pilgrimage" is one of the oldest religious rituals in the world (and one of a handful of circular pilgrimages). It is a rite of passage for Shingon Buddhists, and a UNESCO World Heritage site protected for its cultural importance to Japan.

Located in the North Atlantic Ocean, where it is protected by the outstretched "leg" of its more famous mainland neighbour, Hiroshima, Shikoku is the smallest of Japan's four main islands. The island itself is made up of four now-united provinces – Ehime, Kagawa, Kōchi and Tokushima, giving it its name, *Shikoku*, meaning "four countries". An island of incredible natural beauty, Shikoku is complete with hot springs, vine bridges, sweeping valleys, colossal cedar trees, botanical gardens, mountains and, perhaps most famously, Chichibugahama beach. However, the reason we're here is that it is located just a short (spiritual) stroll away from the beaten path: the Henro.

The "88 Temple Pilgrimage" is one of the oldest pilgrimages in the world – and one that attracts just as many non-religious pilgrims as it does religious – with many thousands of Japanese as well as foreign tourists venturing along the trail to soak up the spiritual energy that the island seems to have on tap.

A power spot is one that refreshes the spirit and inspires feelings of awe. And Shikoku has them in abundance. The island itself is one big power spot, of course, but there are a few sites where the energy is considered to be concentrated: Kannon-ji, Mount Shippo, Oboke Gorge, Tojindaba, Usubae Cove, Giant Rocks of Mount Tateishi, Tojin Spoiled Field Ruins and

Zentsuji Temple are the most significant. The latter is cherished as the birthplace of the Kōbō Daishi, the founder of Shingon Buddhism in 794 CE, and is the head temple of the sect. Shingon is one of the major schools of Buddhism in Japan, with the Henro at the centre of its spiritual rituals to reach nirvana.

The 88 temples along the route of the pilgrimage were important to Kōbō Daishi, all being places where he meditated or spent time during his life. For pilgrims of Shingon Buddhism, it is believed that if you complete the entire route it will purify your soul, with the feast of natural surroundings feeding your eyes. There are many non-religious reasons to complete the route, too. And in recent years it is been transforming itself into a spiritual, healing journey, where wanderers can get away from the stresses of modern life and first lose themselves in reflection and follow up with a walk into self-discovery. The route takes about 40 days on foot to complete, which should give visitors more than enough time to reflect, consider and improve.

Opposite: Most pilgrims begin their route at Temple 1: Ryōzenji, and proceed clockwise to finish at Temple 88: Ōkuboji. This method is called *jun-uchi*. You can go counter-clockwise – *gyaku-uchi*. There is no rule as to which order you follow when you visit the temples.

Western Wall

THE HOLIEST JEWISH SITE IN THE WORLD, FROM THE TIME OF KING HEROD

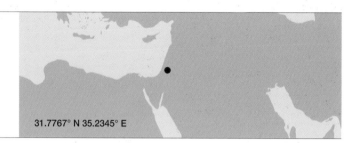

- ✳ Israel
- ✝ Multifaith
- 🏛 19 BCE
- 👥 2.5 million
- 🗓 All year round
- 📍 488 x 19 m (1,601 x 62 ft)

31.7767° N 35.2345° E

This seemingly simple, exposed section of an ancient wall is a site of huge significance for multiple religions. In an area known for conflict and controversy, the wall is a haven of prayer and worship, and a place for people from all nations and all religions to have their worries listened to.

The tradition at the Western Wall, for all believers regardless of their faith and origin, is to write a prayer down on a piece of paper, roll it up and cram it into the wall. Millions come every year to undergo this gentle, peaceful ritual. Prior to the Covid-19 pandemic, it is estimated that more than 2 million people per month were visiting.

The Western Wall is part of what was one of the most important religious buildings in the world, the truly magnificent Second Temple. It was ordered to be built by King Herod on the perimeter of the holy Temple Mount around 19 BCE, and parts of it still stand to today, testament to outstanding construction techniques and the solidity of the rock. In fact, there is a whole lot more of the wall below ground: around a further 17 more courses, roughly one half of the wall's entire height. It is reported that the Second Temple was not completed during Herod's lifetime, and construction continued long after his death in 4 BCE. The temple was destroyed by the Romans in 70 CE, alongside most of the city of Jerusalem.

Known as *Ha-Kotel Ha-ma'aravi* in the Hebrew language, the Western Wall was known as the "Wailing Wall" for a long time, although that description has become less popular and is seen as a negative way of referring to the structure, as it was based around tourists who witnessed the suffering of members of the Jewish faith as they prayed.

Situated right next to the Dome of the Rock and Al-Aqçsā Mosque, the wall has been the scene of some conflict and controversial decisions, as followers of different faiths have sought to defend what they see as their own holy territories. As the American author Edward Wilmot Blyden (*From West Africa to Palestine*) wrote in 1866, "No site in Jerusalem affected me more than the Western Wall." Prayers and devotion have been present in this site for thousands of years, however, and archaeologists who were investigating deep in the foundations found evidence of Roman involvement in the site from a very early time.

The temple that the Wall formed part of gets multiple mentions in the Bible, and a particular point is made for foreigners to be allowed – encouraged even – to visit the site and be made welcome: "As for the foreigner who does not belong to your people Israel but has come from a distant land because of your great name and your mighty hand and your outstretched arm…"

In fact, the Bible encourages everyone, regardless of creed, colour and status, to visit the Western Wall.

Opposite: The Western Wall is made of limestone that was quarried from the ground more than 1,000 years ago. In less hot countries such rock would have denigrated more quickly, but heat does not damage it as much as rain or pollution.

CHAPTER 4

Natural
Wonders

Some spiritual places were built thousands of years ago,
some much more recently. But many on this amazing
planet were created by the forces of science and nature
(or a variety of greater beings, depending on what you
believe) and were discovered, adapted and preserved by
humankind. Here, we look at a selection of the most
incredible wonders from the wonderful world around us.

Adam's Peak

THE TAKE-OFF AND LANDING SPOT OF THE GODS

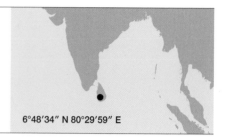

⊛ Sri Lanka

✝ Christian, Buddhist, Hindu, Islam

🏛 2,500 years

👥 20,000

📅 January–July

📍 2,243 m (7,359 ft) (height)

6°48'34" N 80°29'59" E

At the top of the consecrated trek up this conical mountain is a "holy footprint" – a rock indentation imbued with an deep spiritual importance that is shared by each of the world's main religions. It is one of a handful destinations on earth to unite them all.

Emerging out of the lush green jungles of central Sri Lanka and pointing, rather aptly, towards the heavens, Adam's Peak, or *Sri Pada* as it is known locally, is the spiritual home of a temple that houses the "sacred footprint". This religious rock formation is believed by many – Christians and Muslims among them – to be Adam's first footprint on earth after he was banished from paradise, the Garden of Eden. Disciples of Islam also believe it is the solitary indentation of Adam, the same first man and prophet of Christianity, where he stood on one foot for 1,000 years as penance for his exile from heaven.

It is also believed to be the final footprint of Buddha before he stepped up into the light as he attained enlightenment and reached nirvana. For disciples of Hinduism, the name of the mountain is *Sivan Adi Padham*, a name that describes the creation dance of the god Shiva, who founded the world and left a footprint in its wake.

For the many followers of these four world religions, ascending Adam's Peak and praying at the edge of the footprint is a pilgrimage that is hugely significant to their faith and beliefs, and has been happening – for Buddhists at least – since 300 years before Christ. It was not until the 16th century that Christians claimed the site for Adam, following the arrival of Portuguese explorer Marco Polo, who came to Sri Lanka in 1505 and made Portugal the first European nation to rule the island (Lanka is a word that simply means 'island' in English).

The footprint that is set into the boulder at the summit would belong to a being with very large feet (when compared to humans at least), because it measures in at 1.8 metres (5 ft 11 in.) in length. Today it is preserved in a shrine, allowing visitors to pass, or worship as they see fit.

In the time before the worldwide spread of Christianity, Buddhism and Hinduism, the mountain's peak was worshipped by the indigenous people of Sri Lanka, known as the Veddas. They called their mountain Samanala Kanda, after Saman, one of the four guardian deities of the island.

There are various routes for pilgrims to follow up the mountain, some more direct and popular than others. And there is a number of interesting sites and monuments dotted around those trails, not least of which is the Peace Pagoda, which was built by the religious movement known as Nipponzan Myohoji in 1978. This small Buddhist order is most famous for constructing a number of these peace pagodas in various countries around the world. This reiterates just how many of the world's religions venerate Adam's Peak as a significant site.

Opposite: To reach the peak of Adam's summit, pilgrims need to prepare to ascend more than 5,500 steps to reach enlightenment. Some make this trip at night, and there is a bell on the summit, traditionally rung by pilgrims who have made their way to the top.

Byron Bay

AUSTRALIA'S SHINING STAR OF SPIRITUALITY

⊛ Australia

† Aboriginal

🏛 20,000 BCE

👥 2 million

🗓 All year round

🗺 12,406 km² (4,789 sq. mi.)

28°38'35" S 153°36'54" E

Cape Byron, home to Byron Bay, is the most easterly tip of Australia (next stop, Chile). It is the nation's first sunspot to receive the daily illuminating luminescence of our home star. As such – and for a variety of other reasons – it's a spellbinding place to indulge your spiritual senses.

Byron Bay is revered as Australia's spiritual and healing capital. And it's not just famous locally, but globally, too, and for plenty of reasons. Due to its geographical location – almost precisely halfway along Australia's eastern side – the town of Byron Bay has long been a meeting place for all sorts of people. The oldest being the northern and southern tribes of the Bundjalung Nation, Aboriginals comprising of the Arakwal Bumberlin people, who have gathered at Byron Bay for more than 20,000 years for sacred ceremonies and healing purposes, as well as for fishing, dancing, birthing rituals, spiritual retreats and Dreaming. The latter of these is the Aboriginal term to describe telling and recreating of their creation stories and beliefs held by different tribes. In the Bundjalung language of the Arakwal Bumberlin, the area encompassing today's Byron Bay was known as *Cavanbah,* or "meeting place".

And today as it was centuries ago this sunny, hospitable hotspot is still revered as the gold standard of meeting places. For a new generation of tourists it is famed for its beaches, surfers, sunshine and centre point on the Gold Coast. But Byron Bay is more than that, it is a veritable melting pot for travellers from around the world, an epicentre for Australia's counterculture that unites backpackers, tourists and new-age hippies, and it is a magnet for spiritualists, healers and enthusiasts seeking to find, lose and restore themselves in yoga, reiki, meditation and wellness.

And it is not just the healthy air and the sunny beaches that contribute tho the feeling of wellbeing in the area. Byron Bay is often spoken of in regard to its substratum of obsidian, which was created by ancient volcanic activity. There are some who believe that this ancient, igneous rock infuses the bay and surrounding area with an energizing, all-powerful force. We can employ this volcanic glass as a holistic healing substance that, it is said, can cleanse, purge and protect the minds from evil spirits and ideas.

It is also believed by some that Byron Bay is a junction for song lines (known as ley lines in the UK), connecting the channels of earth's energies together into a powerful vortex of healing. There is a marine park, a national park and multiple nature reserves, providing a direct connection to nature in various forms. And whether you are in Byron Bay for a wellbeing retreat, a dip in the ocean, a stroll in the hills or simply to meet people, talk and have fun; no matter what mystical, psychic or metaphysical belief bought you to this place on that can feel like the very edge of civilization, Byron Bay has something for everyone – spirituality of all shapes and sizes in abundance.

Opposite: Named by Captain Cook, who sailed by in 1770, Byron Bay is not named after the English poet Lord Byron as many first think, but rather his grandfather, Vice-Admiral John Byron.

Cape Reinga

ANCIENT MEETING PLACE FOR MAORI SPIRITS

⊛ New Zealand

✝ Māori

🏛 1300

🐛 120,000

📅 Summer (in NZ)

📍 100 hectares (247 acres)

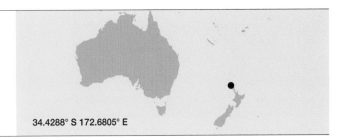

34.4288° S 172.6805° E

Cape Reinga is perfectly positioned for the native Māori people of New Zealand, who consider this nearly northernmost peak to be the most spiritually sacred site in their entire homeland.

For the near-million Māori people who live on the beautiful island-nation of New Zealand, there is nowhere more spiritual than Cape Reinga. Known as *Te Rerenga Wairua* – "the leaping-off place of spirits" – Cape Reinga is the sacred meeting place where the Pacific Ocean to the east and the Tasman Sea to the west unite. In the minds of the deeply spiritual Māori, this union of two bodies of water represents the symbolic coming together of life energy: the two seas, one male (Rehua), one female (Whitirea), crashing into each other to give life to the world. It is this process that the Māori call *Te Moana-a-Rehua* – "the meeting of the seas". The word *Māori* itself means "life force" – and this baptism of water is blessed by Tangaroa, the "god of the sea" and a central figurehead in Māori origin stories. But while the Cape itself is the site of birth and rebirth, it is also a place that pays tribute to the act of passing on, relating also to the cycle of life. For the Māori, *Reinga* also has the meaning "underworld", serving as a portal to a place beyond the known.

According to the many Māori creation stories that have been handed down for generations, the spirits of departed tribe members meet at the Cape's head to transcend the physical realm of earth before embarking on the journey back to their spiritual homeland, the ancestral and heavenly Hawaiki.

All along the coastline, found at the tip of the cape, visitors will find the red-flowered Pohutukawa tree. These sacred trees, through their roots, which reach deep and long into the symbolic waters of the Pacific, are the entrances to the underworld. This particular tree species is today around 800 years old, which is an emblematic age for the Māori, as they are approximately the same age as the Māoris' tenure of New Zealand. When the first tribes arrived here from Polynesia, by canoe, around 700 years ago, the first sight of new land would have featured these strange, red trees. They would have resembled a glowing light, beckoning the arrivals to their new home. And like the soon-to-be entrancing Māori legends, these young saplings would have only just begun their adventures at the Cape.

Visitors to the area today find an ostensibly barren shore, with a lone lighthouse shining as a warning to ships that navigate the cold seas. But there is much to do to experience for yourself the deeply spiritual nature of the land as it meets the ocean. There are many miles of trails to follow, many beaches to admire and many forests to walk through and wonder at. And on a misty day you can really feel the spiritual nature of land, sea and air as they mix together, existing as one, as they have on this point for millions of years.

Opposite: Tangaroa, the god of the sea, is the spiritual son of Papatūānuku, the earth mother, and Ranginui, the sky father, two supreme creation "gods" of Māori culture. Looking out at the sea and sky from Cape Reinga, it's easy to see why.

Crater Lake

A VISION QUEST IN AMERICA'S SACRED PACIFIC NORTHWEST

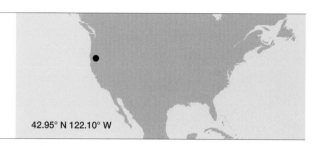

- ✴ USA
- ✝ Native American (Klamath)
- 🏛 5,000 BCE
- 👤 750,000
- 📅 July–September
- 🗺 53 km² (20.6 sq. mi.)

42.95° N 122.10° W

Around 7,700 years ago, before the eruption of Oregon's 3,657-metre (12,000-ft) tall super-volcano Mount Mazama, the Klamath tribe ruled this picturesque patch of earth. When Mazama blew its top and collapsed in on itself, it left behind a 53 square kilometre (20.6 sq. mi.) crater that became known by the Klamath as *Giiwas*: "a sacred place". How right they were.

Before its violent demise, Mount Mazama was an important symbol to the Klamath, a Native American tribe based around the Pacific Northwest in the states we know as Oregon and Washington today. These peoples' spiritual beliefs told of stories that the mountain's destruction was because of the heroic battle between good and evil: the heavenly god of the sky, Skell, and the evil spirit of the below world, Llao. Skell defeated Llao by driving him downwards, then collapsing the mountain on top of him, imprisoning him forever underground. In order to ensure that peace and tranquillity endured above this dark place, Skell covered the land with the beguiling deep blue and super-clear crystal waters that visitors have since enjoyed for centuries. In doing so, Skell created America's deepest lake, a 592-metre (1,942-ft) deep oasis that is truly unlike any other on its own continent – or further afield.

What is incredible – from a purely geological perspective at least – is that no rivers or water sources flow in to or out of the lake. The natural evaporation of the lake's surface water by the sun is topped up by only rain and snow – it is situated in one of the snowiest (13 metres [42 ft] of annual snowfall) and wettest places in the United States – which goes to ensure that all of the fresh lake water in Crater Lake is fully – and quite naturally – replaced every 250 years.

To Oregon's Klamath people and their ancestors, Crater Lake was and remains to be a deeply special place where they are able to connect to their spirit world through vision quests, a traditional rite-of-passage ceremony that leads to a life-transforming experience. Vision quests include puberty rituals, acceptance initiations, spirit approval/blessings, and isolation challenges. Some vision quests can be incredibly difficult tasks that require extreme levels of courage and skill. Those individuals who are successful in their quests often become regarded as possessing greater spiritual powers, and may rise through the ranks in a tribe.

Many of these trials would take place in or near the lake, so today, as it has been for several thousand years, the Klamath hold Crater Lake dear as a sacred and profound place that binds them to the planet.

Popular with tourists, locals and scientists for varying reasons, the Crater Lake National Park (established in 1902) is located in the Jewel Valley in Oregon, and is revered as supremely special by newcomers and those who have been visiting for centuries.

Opposite: In the centre of Crater Lake are two small and strange-shaped islands, Wizard Island, a large cinder cone, and Phantom Ship, a natural rock pillar.

Devils Tower

A SACRED IGNEOUS INTRUSION RISING FROM THE PLAINS

 USA

 Native American

250 BCE

1 million

All year round (bar June)

264 m (867 ft) (height)

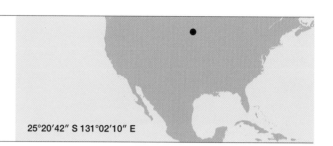

25°20′42″ S 131°02′10″ E

Rising from the Wyoming plains like a surreal sculpture, Devils Tower has been around a lot longer than humankind. And this mysterious structure has been revered and worshipped for thousands of years. More recently, it has become a Mecca for climbers, keen to test their skills on the ancient rock.

Thrust to the surface of the planet millions of years ago, Devils Tower is a butte (see Monument Valley on page 150 for more examples). It was most likely formed underground from molten rock before being pushed up into the surrounding sedimentary rock, where it underwent a process of hardening over many years. To delve a little into the science, the rock is phonolite porphyry, which is similar to granite. The butte itself is not hollow, but solid. However, the "columns" on the edges have been known to separate from the body and tumble; however this has not happened for many hundreds of years.

Devils Tower was not formally named in the English language until 1875, when Colonel Richard Irving Dodge was on an expedition through the Black Hills mountain range, located in Wyoming, close to the border with South Dakota. The name "Devils Tower" was recorded by the party, further stating that the natives "call this shaft the Bad God's Tower." Unfortunately, it is likely that this was simply a mistranslation that was made at the time and that stuck, for many of the Native names for the tower referenced bears. For example, it was referred to as "Bear Lodge" in early maps of the area, and was so referred by the indigenous population. This is a bone of contention to this day, with Native tribes still trying to have the name of the butte amended, claiming – not without justification – that Devils Tower is profoundly disrespectful to their sacred site.

The first ever official national monument in the United States of America, Devils Tower was proclaimed as such by President Theodore Roosevelt in 1906 – the original apostrophe being dropped at this point as well.

Those lucky enough to get to the top of the impressive naturally formed tower (by climbing – there's no staircase, lift or cable car) find a surprisingly large open and relatively flat space (it is very gently domed), around 91 by 55 metres (300 ft by 180 ft). The low number of visitors to the summit means wildlife is able to thrive, with chipmunks, mice, rats and snakes living among the cactus, grass and rock that adorn the plateau.

The incredible tower has long been an important landmark for the indigenous peoples of the area, most of them associating it with bears: the Cheyenne call it Bear Lodge, the Mandan Bear's Hat and the Arapaho Bear's Tipi. Many have legends that involve Devils Tower, with one such story claiming that the gashes on the side of the tower were created by a giant bear.

Opposite: Devils Tower enjoyed worldwide fame in the 1970s when it featured strongly in Stephen Spielberg's enormously popular movie *Close Encounters of the Third Kind.* In it an alien mothership comes down to earth – with Devils Tower being the meeting point.

Es Vedrà

A FLOATING FORTRESS OF SOLITUDE

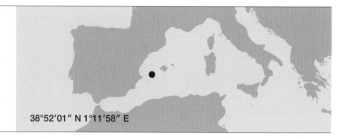

- ✳ Spain
- ✝ New Age
- ▥ 800 BCE
- ♟ 4.8 million
- ▦ June–August
- ◉ <.5 km² (<.2 sq. mi.)

38°52'01" N 1°11'58" E

Floating solo and uninhabited in the Balearic Sea, 3.2 km (2 miles) off the west coast of Ibiza, Es Vedrá, to those who seek it, is a new age dream pilgrimage… and a postcard-perfect vision of heaven on earth.

As the supposed site of immense magnetic energy, it's no surprise that millions of free-spirited travellers are drawn to the healing power of this magical, monolithic limestone rock formation; the source, some say, of Ibiza's world-renowned spiritual and creative energy. It is, indeed, a stunning marvel of nature, a sight to experience.

At 413 metres (1,355 ft) high, this beautiful landmark towers triumphantly into the sky, a beacon of geological prowess, offering a majestic backdrop for both a sunset and sunrise. This is especially apparent when it is seen from the (relatively) nearby Cala D'Hort, Ibiza's most esteemed beach (out of 57 to choose from), which is the envy of many a tourist hotspot.

But Es Vedrá is more than just the ideal place to soak in the sun or bask in some all-natural spiritual energy. It is also perfectly geographically positioned for it to be the home of many legends and myths. According to folklore, the island is the tip of the submerged, ancient, lost city of Atlantis. The mythical place that was built by Poseidon, the Ancient Greek god of the sea, as a symbol of his love for a mortal woman. Of the many Atlantis myths worldwide, it is certainly a contender. Other legends laid at Es Vedrá's doorstep include being the residence of the sirens who attempted to lure Odysseus and his crew to a watery grave in Homer's *The Odyssey*. To ensure the failure to temptation of the sirens' song, Odysseus instructs his crew to tie him securely to the mast of his ship as they stuff their ears

with beeswax and promise not to release him however much he begs and pleads. That knowledge was a gift from the nymph Circe, whom Odysseus lives with for a while.

Another ancient myth associated with the island is that is was the birthplace of Tanit (or Tinnit), the renowned Phoenician goddess who was much worshipped in parts of western Europe – particularly around the Mediterranean and Balearic seas and north Africa before the 1st century BCE.

Myth, legend and story aside, the island of Es Vedrá is a deeply spiritual location, and ideal for those looking for solitude in the sun. And, certainly, as the sun sets on the *Torre des Savinar* ("Pirate's Tower"), viewed from Cala D'Hort on neighbouring Ibiza, it's impossible not to feel some sort of spiritual energy pulsating from the rock.

Visiting the island itself (now a designated nature reserve) is very difficult, and you would need special permissions to dock and visit the shore – both of which are notoriously difficult to obtain. But it is not necessary to set foot on the island to see and feel its power. It is relatively simple to go on a boat trip that sails around the island slowly, giving a feel of just how remote this sun-drenched and wind-whipped place is.

Opposite: As the sun goes down on Es Vedrà it is hard not to feel the spiritual energy that emanates from the vast rock in the sea.

Futami Okitama Shrine

MARRIAGE ROCKS REINFORCED BY THE GODS

- ✳ Japan
- ✝ Shinto
- 🏛 2000 BCE
- 👥 2.4 million
- 🗓 21 June
- 🗺 N/A

34.5089° N, 136.7878° E

Under the watchful gaze of Mount Fuji, the Futami Okitama shrine is a Shinto temple in the city of Ise, in Mie Prefecture. It is the most famous example of *Meoto-iwa* – the union of two blessed rocks, one large and one small, wedded together in holy matrimony.

In Japan, there are more than 100,000 Shinto sanctuaries, with several dozen *Meoto-iwa* sites, but the Futami Okitama Shrine is the most famous. For thousands of years, the waters of Futami have set the scene of *misogi*, a ritual water immersion that is similar to a Christian baptism. This is performed prior to a pilgrimage to Japan's most celebrated and ancient Shinto shrine complexes, the nearby Ise Jingu. They are extremely large, roughly the same size as the city centre of Paris.

According to Shinto beliefs, the sacred stones that stand in the sea here embody the creator kami, as well as Izanagi and Izanami, who, according to Japanese folklore, birthed the isles of Japan as well as many of the kami (sacred spirits) and even represent the earthly marriage of man and woman. Known as Tateishi and Nejiriwa (husband and wife), the two huge rocks are visible at both high and low tides, despite being some 700 metres (2,296 ft) offshore. The two are bound together by a thick ceremonial rope, as are all other *meoto-iwa* ("married couple") rocks. The rope is known as *shimenawa*, and made of a particular type of heavy rice straw. The rope is also seen as sacred and is reattached to the rocks three times a year: December (before the New Year), May and September. Each *shimenawa* rope is custom-built and made up of five strands, each of which has a weight of 40 kilograms (88 lb). The Ikawara rock types are the region's principal spiritual site, as they embody Izanagi and Izanami deities.

In recent years, the shrines have blossomed as a romantic destination for newly married couples to visit and celebrate (or re-celebrate) their union – and take a photograph that they will treasure forever. They believe that Izanagi and Izanami will bless them with their love, too.

As you would expect in a country that adheres strictly to tradition and heritage, the upkeep of the rocks is taken incredibly seriously. There is a National Married Couple Rocks Summit Liaison Council, formed of representatives from ten different prefectures, who come together on a regular basis and discuss the rocks and their cultural, spiritual and religious impact.

Not all rocks are equal, and although the Futami Okitami rocks are covered by the sea, there are plenty that aren't. There is a pair of rocks in Kariuzawa that are land-based, and another pair in Muoro City that perch on the side of a cliff. Whatever the location, however picturesque, the rocks are always respected and looked after by the community around them – as an old married couple themselves, ones that have really stood the test of time.

Opposite: This romantic spot is recognized as one of Japan's 23 UNESCO World Heritage Sites, and the rocks have a magical presence whether viewed by day in the sunshine, or at night by shimmering moonlight.

Joshua Tree

BIBLICAL ROOTS IN WEST COAST DESERT SAND

⊛ USA

✝ Native American

▥ 2,500 BCE

⚇ 2.4 million

⊛ March–May; Oct/Nov

⊛ 3,218 km² (1,242 sq. mi.)

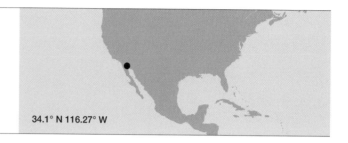

34.1° N 116.27° W

For more than 5,000 years, the Serrano, Mojave, Cahuilla and Chemehuevi Native peoples have imbued this dual desert landscape ecosystem (Mojave mixed with Colorado) with mystical stories told under the watchful eye of the Milky Way.

Welcome to the best place on earth to get lost – America's West Coast wilderness. This hallowed ground covers more than 3,000 square kilometres (1,000 sq. mi.) and can be found almost exactly halfway between the cities of Los Angeles and San Diego – the nation's most famous star-obsessed hotspots. (The view of the stars from Joshua Tree is even better, however, having been designated a Dark Sky Park. It's so far removed – more than 200 kilometres (124 miles) – from the light pollution of modern life and cities that the Milky Way comes out to play every clear night, a fact that the Mojave people have blended into their spiritual myths and legends.)

It is named after the now-famous yucca plant (*Yucca brevifolia*) – not a tree – that punctuates the earth, a species native only to the Mojave Desert. The local Cahuilla Nation – one of the original peoples of this land – refer to the trees as *humwichawa*.

However, the famous "Joshua" moniker originates from the first Mormons who made their way across the Colorado river and began to settle in the region between Los Angeles and Las Vegas in the 1850s. The name "Joshua" was given when those early Mormon pioneers agreed that the branches of the yucca looked similar to arms outstretched in supplication (Mormons prayed then with arms outstretched towards the sky, not clasped together, mimicking Christ on the cross). The Mormon settlers believed the tree was guiding them westward just as the Joshua of the Bible, Moses' successor, helped guide him towards the promised land, Jericho. Furthermore the name "Joshua" originally comes from the Hebrew name *Yehoshua*, meaning "God is deliverance".

Today, these trees help to guide travellers and tourists towards their various destinations, and they have become a world-famous icon of the desert's spirituality; the ability of those hardy trees to survive in drought and desolation serves as a metaphor for those seeking some salvation.

It is the Joshua tree's capacity to thrive here that explains why this desert landscape has been long revered as a place of huge spiritual significance, a magnet for energy vortices and a place for individuals to channel the desert's energy into their own spiritual healing and quest for inner peace.

Today, the Joshua Tree National Park and its surroundings represent a veritable haven, for a multitude of spiritual retreats and wellness centres that offer many things from enhanced and advanced yoga, hypnotherapy and meditation healing, to lessons in "mental physics" and more, for those in search of something different – and special – to stir into their spiritual soup.

Opposite: The rock band U2 named their 1987 album *The Joshua Tree*, combining spiritual imagery of their religious upbringing with their fascination with "mythical America". It sold 25 million copies, and became one of the world's bestselling, and critically acclaimed, records.

Lake Atitlán

AN ELEVATED LAGOON AS DEEP AS IT IS DIVINE

- ✳ Guatemala
- ✝ Mayan
- 🏛 2,000 years
- 👥 1.5 million
- 📅 January–March
- 🗺 135 km² (52 sq. mi.)

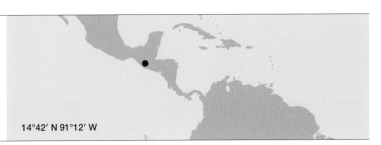

14°42′ N 91°12′ W

Guatemala's volcanic Lake Atitlán is the nation's most visited natural tourist attraction, a heaven on earth enriched by the ancient traditions of the Mayan tribes, who have worshipped its ancestral history and hallowed its healing properties for more than 1,000 years.

Located in southwest Guatemala, in the highlands of the famed Sierra Madre mountain range, the lake is surrounded on all sides by three dramatic volcanoes – Atitlán, Tolimán and San Pedro – known as the Three Giants. It is this positioning that has allowed a rich and diverse community of peoples to encircle the lake's perimeter, with the volcanoes offering fertile soils as rich and deep as the ancient stories generations have passed on about the lake. The esteemed author Aldous Huxley was so taken with this bountiful body of water he described it perfectly: "The limit of the permissibly picturesque, like Lake Como but with the additional embellishments of several immense volcanoes – it really is *too much* of a good thing". We couldn't agree more.

Borrowing its name from the Nahuatl language to mean "between waters", the lake has been an important home for Mayan tribes, who believe its cavernous waters offer a portal to the sacred their underworld, Xibalba. According to the Mayan's beliefs, the sacred and divine emerge from the ground, not from the heavens above. The Mayans believed the lake had a powerful energy that protected and enriched the land and its people and were unshaken in their stance that the lake is one of the world's three great energy vortexes. (The others being Machu Picchu in Peru and the Pyramids of Giza in Egypt). The Mayans attribute the birth of the lake to spiritual events that are explained in the *Popol Vuh* – the Book of the Community – the creation stories of the Guatemalan Mayans.

Other, more scientifically based stories of the lake's origins hold it to be volcanic, when around 85,000 years ago a super volcano named Los Chocoyos erupted in an event so massive it blew itself into pieces. That was an event now considered to be the greatest volcanic eruption of the last 100,000 years, and it created the enormous caldera on which the lake's deep waters now rest, as well as much of the rest of the landscape.

Lake Atitlán also has a rich spiritual history. On the north side of the lake live the Kakchiguel-speaking Mayans. On the south, the Tz'utuhil. Over the centuries they have fought to be sole caretakers of the lake, fighting over its powerful energy. Both sides speak of a legend like *Romeo and Juliet* – once a Kakchiguel and Tz'utuhil fell in love, and knowing their affair was doomed, they drowned together in the lake's deep waters, their deaths finally bringing the two warring communities together. Their love cleansed the waters and gave it the healing qualities enjoyed by those who believe today.

Opposite: Lake Atitlán's true beauty is more than its impossible natural style. It has substance, too. It is the deepest body of water in Central America, with its bottom more than 325 metres (1,100 ft) below.

Lake Titicaca

THE INCAN BIRTHPLACE OF THE SUN

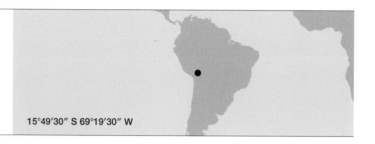

⊛ Peru/Bolivia

✝ Inca

🏛 1600 BCE

👥 1 million

📅 May/October

🗺 8,300 km² (3,204 sq. mi.)

15°49'30" S 69°19'30" W

The largest lake in South America, the highest lake in the world, and one of the most ancient bodies of water on earth, (three million years old and counting), Lake Titicaca's crystal-clear waters are as pure as its spiritual origins.

High in the Andes, on the border between Peru and Bolivia (Peru to the west and Bolivia to the east), Lake Titicaca is a sight for sore eyes, from its underwater Inca temple to its shimmery freshwater surface. A vast body of water, about 80 kilometres (50 miles) across at its widest point and the final destination for more than 25 rivers, it is easy to understand why the Tiwanku, then Incas and now today's ancestral cultures have worshipped this imposing, ancient lake for many thousands of years; and why it is also popular with tourists.

From above, the distinct shape of the lake resembles that of a puma – go check – the Mesoamerican spirit animal that also gives the lake its name; Titicaca, derived from *Titi-Khar-ka* from the local Aymara language, which translates into English as "rock of the puma". And as they did with the puma, the Incas and local civilizations that inhabited the region revered the lake as magical, calling it the birthplace of the sun god, Inti, and his father, Viracocha, the creator god, when they rose out of the lake to bring light to the darkness. Since then, for Incas, the lake has been the centre of their entire cosmos. These ancient peoples also worshipped the idea that other divine ancestors – such as Pachamama, or Mother Nature – rose out of Titicaca possessed with celestial powers that infused the waters with vast spiritual and healing gifts. In annual festivals celebrating the lake and Inca deities, such as January's Fiesta de la Santa Tierra, and November's Puno week,

the Incas' modern ancestors continue to make offerings to the water, which many believe once included human and animal sacrifices. As you would imagine with such a significant source of food, travel and trade, more than 180 ruins and monuments remain in the region surrounding Lake Titicaca. One of the most dramatic and significant being the remains of a large, ancient underwater temple complex thought to be more than 1,500 years old. It was built by the Tiwanaku people – a pre-Inca civilization – and was discovered submerged in the lake alongside a long road, a wall and an ancient terrace for crops, in 2000. Explorers followed an old trail that seemed to plunge into the lake and were rewarded with the significant find.

Living in the heart of the lake, still to this day, on the famous floating islands are the Uros, an indigenous people (around 1,200 population) from Peru and Bolivia who built 120 football-field-sized floating islands by hand, using entirely a thick reed, known as *totora*. These man-made wonders – and Uru culture – have existed for a millennia, deeply believing in the sacred energy of the lake, and co-existed with mainland Incas with little conflict.

Opposite: The lake's largest island is Isla del Sol (Island of the Sun). Many ancient ruins are still here, including the Sacred Rock, a labyrinthine stone structure and a shrine to the spot where Incas believed their sun god, Inti, rose from the lake.

Little Manitou Lake

THE HIDDEN HEALING POWERS OF CANADA'S "DEAD SEA"

⊛ Canada

✝ Native Canadian

🏛 8000 BCE

👥 250,000

📅 Summer (for bathing)

📍 13.4 km² (5.2 sq. mi.)

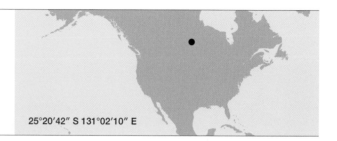

25°20'42" S 131°02'10" E

The mineral-rich waters (and mud) of Little Manitou Lake have been identified and used for many years for their restorative qualities. Famed in the local area for once curing smallpox, there is more to this lake than meets the eye…

Tucked way in the Canadian province of Saskatchewan is the small saltwater lake named Little Manitou Lake. In an area rich with water, there are more than 1,000 lakes in the province, but only one that is so rich in minerals that it gleams a metallic bronze and works like a natural floatation device. Little Manitou Lake – like many of the lakes around it – was formed by glaciers receding in the ice age. However – not like many of the lakes around it – Little Manitou Lake has a very high salinity content that makes it unique in the area. With a level five times greater than the ocean and a little under half of what is found in the Dead Sea that borders Israel and Jordan in the Middle East, Little Manitou Lake is totally unique. As in the Dead Sea, swimmers in Little Manitou Lake are pleasantly surprised by the added buoyancy – although unsuspecting canoeists find themselves prone to capsizing due to their craft's riding much higher in the water than usual.

The lake has been revered by local tribes for centuries, but almost nothing has been recorded or handed down orally until around the last 200 years or so. The most recent – and most famous – legend goes along these lines: a group of local native Assiniboine people were affected by a major smallpox epidemic and were forced to flee from their base towards the south. As they travelled further their condition worsened and one was forced to abandon two of his companions who could walk no further. He arrived at the edge of a lake (Little Manitou Lake as

it turned out), and, parched and feverish, drank from the cool water. He then slept, and when he awoke he was completely free of any symptoms. He went back for his two friends, who made it to the lake and did the same – the magical effect of the waters was replicated and all three were cured. This is generally accepted to have caused a slow but steady influx of locals at first, then visitors from further afield.

From the 1930s, Manitou became an actual tourist resort, with thousands of visitors, from local holidaymakers wanting to play in the water to well-being pilgrims who came for the water's restorative qualities and peaceful surroundings.

These days, the waters and the mud beneath them are scientifically proven to have many minerals and salts in them, and visitors claim to have been cured of a wide variety of illnesses and ailments, including skin conditions, arthritis, joint pains and many more besides. And although some of these seem a bit unlikely, there is plenty of evidence that it's certainly better to have a dip in the lake's soothing waters than not. Entire industries have built up around the healing waters, from well-being retreats and spas to exports of masks and lotions.

Opposite: With a pH of 1.06, the waters of the lake are much more buoyant than regular seawater, ensuring a constant stream of visitors throughout the year.

Monument Valley

EARTH, WIND AND FIRE INSPIRE A VALLEY OF MONOLITHS

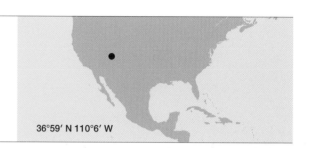

- ✳ USA
- ✝ Native American (Navajo)
- ☷ Circa 1000
- 👥 350,000
- 📅 March–August
- 🗺 2,848 km² (1,100 sq. mi.)

36°59' N 110°6' W

Uniting the Four Corners of the American Southwest, a place where Arizona, Utah, Colorado and New Mexico join at the seams, Monument Valley is considered so uniquely American that when John Wayne first set eyes on it, he said, "So, this is where God put the West". But, this land is not cowboy country…

Yá'át'ééh. That's "hello" in Navajo. Monument Valley belongs to the Navajo (or Diné as they call themselves), a Native American people, more than 170,000 of whom call this home. This world famous, sun-soaked, red-sand desert, with a collection of colourful canyons and high desert plains, is more than a valley. It is the largest reservation in the world. It has its own language, its own government and time-zone; and significant cultural identity. Technically, it is not even part of the United States of America, but a sovereign state nearly 3,000 square kilometres (1,000 sq. miles) in size. This mystical, barren landscape is the heart and soul of the sincerely spiritual Navajo, who settled here after the ancient Anasazi, who inhabited the valley for a millennia before them, but vanished within a generation. Nobody is sure as to the reasons why, but a megadrought-enforced exodus offers a plausible reason at least.

For the Navajo and their creation stories, Monument Valley is imbued with magic. The iconic, 50-million-year-old sandstone mesas and buttes that punch through the earth are not just enormous rocks weathered by wind, they are the defeated carcasses of mythological monsters of Navajo legend, killed in epic battles by the Navajo's Holy People. Each monument tells a sacred story that is as fascinating as its ancient geology.

Within a 13-square-kilometre (5-sq.-mile) cluster, the ten most photographed monuments can be found. They are rock formations each as different in shape as the last, and each one named with a title that envisions a spiritual connection to the earth. The most iconic and famous formations, however, are the West Mitten Butte, East Mitten Butte, and Merrick Butte. It is these that are the most photographed too. As tall as the Eiffel Tower, these stunning, free-standing, 300-metre (1,000-ft)-tall monoliths look as if they could have been huge clenched fists punching their way out of the earth.

The Navajo tell ancient tales of two classes of being, the mortal, Earth People and the Holy People – the unseen beings who created the universe. To ensure the Earth People lived in harmony with the world they were protected – or punished – by Mother Earth, Father Sky and the Great Spirit. According to Navajo myths, the buttes were gloves that once fitted the giant fists of the Great Spirit back in the time when Monument Valley was the playground of the Holy People. One day, it is said, the Great Spirit will return to reclaim his mittens.

Monument Valley is a Navajo Tribal Park, falling outside the jurisdiction of the federal US government.

Opposite Above and Below: Monument Valley, in Navajo, is *Tse'Bii'Ndzisgaii* – "Valley of the Rocks". At dawn and dusk, these monoliths glow a breathtaking bright orange.

Mount Kailash

TIBET'S PRECIOUS SNOW JEWEL AND THE WORLD'S HOLIEST MOUNTAIN

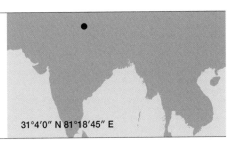

✳	Tibet	👥	3,000+
✝	Hindu, Buddhist, Jain, Bön	📅	April–June; Sept/Oct
🏛	800 BCE	📍	6,638 m (21,778 ft) (height)

31°4'0" N 81°18'45" E

More than a billion Buddhists, Hindus, Jains and Bön, all of whom, despite a different belief system, share the same spiritual truth: Mount Kailash, in western Tibet, is the centre of the universe and the precise spot where heaven says hello to earth.

Its peak may be more than 2,000 metres (6,560ft) shorter than the world's highest mountain, Everest, but make no mistake, Mount Kailash is a towering icon of eastern religious philosophy – *the* portal on earth where the physical and spiritual worlds unite. It is a mountain so sacred to so many that no human has ever, nor will ever, be granted permission to climb to its sanctified summit. To trespass to the top would be to upset the gods of each religion who claim to reside there. According to Tibetan legend, a tantric magician monk, Milarepa, did once ascend the earthly heaven after vanquishing his foe Naro, the rival leader of the Bön, Tibet's folk religion, in an epic battle of sorcery for religious supremacy. When there, Milarepa was reprimanded for disturbing the divine energies resting on the peak. The monk was allowed to return on the condition that he forewarn all others to never climb the mountain again.

As with several other Hindu and Buddhist sites around Asia and the East, Mount Kailash embodies the mystical Mount Meru. In religious texts for both, Meru is the spiritual centre of the universe, a golden mountain with five peaks where all oceans meet. Hindus also claim that Mount Kailash is the primary residence of Shiva, one of the three primordial deities (along with Vishnu and Brahma) and his children, Ganesha and Kartikeya.

Tibetan Buddhists believe Kailash is the home of their deity, Cakrasaṃvara, Shiva's Hindu counterpart, a being who symbolically represents supreme bliss.

According to the scriptures of Jain, an ancient Indian religion separate from Hinduism, Kailash's summit is the sacred spot where the religion's founder, Lord Adinath, was first liberated by enlightenment and reached nirvana. In Bön, Tibet's indigenous religion, Bönpos (disciples) believe that the mountain is the home of their sky goddess, Sipaimen, as well as a celestial stairway to ascend to heaven and the birthplace of their universal creation.

Every year, many thousands of pilgrims make the long walk to Kailash to complete a holy ritual that dates back thousands of years, *Kailash kora*, meaning "revolution". Wuite literally, this means going round in circles. Pilgrims believe that by circumambulating Kailash's 52-kilometres (32-miles)-long base will give them good fortune. Interestingly, Hindus and Buddhists walk around the mountain in a clockwise direction, while Jains and Bönpos stroll in a counterclockwise direction. Each religious pilgrim agrees that a walk around the mountain will wash away sins and please the deities on the peak. It is believed that pilgrims who walk 10 times around the mountain will be saved from hell and those who walk 100 revolutions will attain nirvana and ascend to heaven.

Opposite: *Gang Rinpoche,* the Tibetan name for Mount Kailash, translates as a "precious jewel of snows".

Mount Sinai

FROM UP ON HIGH THE TEN COMMANDMENTS WERE GIVEN TO HUMANKIND

⊛ Egypt

✝ Multifaith

🏛 1313

👥 470,000

📅 October/November

📍 2,285 m (7,497 ft) (height)

28°32′21.9″ N 33°58′31.5″ E

As expected atop a spiritual mountain, the views of the landscape, as well as the rise and fall of the sun each day, are particularly epic. Here at Mount Sinai, in Egypt, however, it isn't just the views that are biblical in nature. Everything else about it is, too.

All of the world's religions hold sacred their own particular mountains. These towers of strengths are the peak of a god's almighty creative might. And in many written texts, such as the Old and New Testament, God and his disciples use imagery of mountains to describe his powers, and use them as powerful metaphors for stability and strength. And while the precise location of the biblical Mount Sinai, as written in the Old Testament, is disputed, its significance is not. In the eyes and minds of Christians, Egypt's Mount Sinai occupies the summit on which Moses received the Ten Commandments from God in the form of two stone tablets. As such, it is a hugely popular pilgrimage site, with as many as 500,000 yearly visitors following in the footsteps of Moses – precisely 3,750 of them (they were carved into the mountain rock by monks in the 16th century) called the Steps of Penitence.

Pilgrims can bathe in the historic spirituality at the peak, where a 300-year-old chapel encloses the rock source which Moses used for the stone tablets, as well as Moses' cave where, it is written, he lived on the top of the mountain. According to the book of Exodus, at the foot of Mount Sinai, where St Catherine's Monastery now resides, Moses first heard the word of God emanating from a burning bush. God instructed Moses to lead the Israelites out of Egypt. Moses travelled to Thebes to convince King Ramses II to release the Israelites to him. The king agreed, and after months of travel, Moses and the Israelites arrived together at the foot of Mount Sinai. With a sudden explosion of thunder and lightning, God summoned Moses to the summit and for 40 days and 40 nights, without eating or drinking water, Moses "wrote on the tablets the words of the covenant – the Ten Commandments", guided by the finger of God. God then instructed Moses to build the Ark of the Covenant, a portable portal to keep the tablets of stone safe. The current location of the Ark is unknown and often disputed, but many believe it resides in the ancient city of Aksum, in Ethiopia (*see* page 16).

After the commandments were written in stone, Moses travelled down the mountain and delivered to the Israelites the Ten Commandments. The rest is religious history.

Anyone who witnesses a sunrise over this beautiful, barren mountain range will never forget it, whatever their beliefs.

Opposite: The 6th-century St Catherine's Monastery at the foot of Mount Sinai is the world's oldest Christian monastery. The monastery is also the oldest library in the world, home to the *Codex Sinaiticus*, the oldest surviving complete manuscript of the New Testament, as well as the earliest known depiction of Jesus as divine.

Nazaré Canyon

A MECCA FOR SURFERS AND SPIRITUAL THRILL SEEKERS

⊛ Portugal

✝ Natural

🏛 2004

👥 400,000

📅 October–March

⚓ 5,000 m (16,400 ft) (depth)

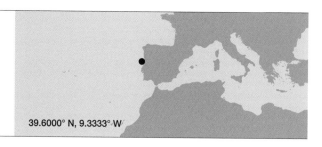

39.6000° N, 9.3333° W

Nazaré, a small fishing village in Portugal, is now a world-famous magnet for big-wave surfers seeking their own form of spiritual sustenance by surfing on a skyscraper-sized sea.

In 2004, the world's most fearless big-wave surfers found themselves a new spiritual home. A place to chase the biggest thrill of all: to catch and survive riding a 30-metre (100-ft) wave – a feat that so far remains (unofficially at least) out of reach. But not for much longer it seems...

The powerful waves in Nazaré, especially on North Beach, are bigger and more unpredictable than anywhere else on earth. And there is a good reason for that. These huge waves are caused by Europe's (and one of the world's) largest underwater canyons, a 5,000-metre (16,000-ft) deep and 230-kilometre (140-mile)-long trench. When a wave originating in the North Atlantic Ocean pushes forward towards the coast it slows down above the canyon. But deep down, inside the canyon, the water retains its speed travelling forward. When the canyon concludes and the two bodies of water collide they create a super wave, which when it hits currents near the shore, transforms into a high-breaking ocean monster. It has proved to be perfect for those seeking a high for all the senses.

The holy grail of big-wave surfing – for its adepts a quest as spiritual as the hunt for Christ's cup – is the 30-metre (100-ft) wave. All that is required is an explorer brave enough to tame one. On 29 October 2020, Portuguese surfer António Laureano made a claim to have ridden the biggest wave ever surfed, a 30.9-metre (100-ft) breaker. Unfortunately this thrilling ride never received official accreditation from Guinness World Records.

One that did, the official tallest tamed wave here, was recognized as a World Record in October 2020, with the official height registered at 26.2 metres (86 ft). Also in 2020, Maya Gabeira broke the record for the biggest wave ever surfed by a woman – her own record as it happens – on a wave out of Nazaré Canyon. This place, off of Europe's west coast, is truly the world centre of big wave riding and many surfers undertake a pilgrimage here in order to partake of their own brand of holy water; it's a bit more bubbly and active than the traditional Christian variety that is blessed by priest.

Surfers describe the fear and adrenaline of riding a big wave at Nazaré canyon, but also the immense connection to the earth, the ocean and the sense of peace that floods their senses right before the wave breaks, an enlightenment that arrives to assist their safe journey towards the shore. As big-wave surf legend Andrew Cotton put it: "Nazaré can be heaven; the best place in the world to surf. Fall off, and it can be... hell."

The Legend of Nazaré occurred in 1182 on the cliffs above the sea; today's legends take place in the water.

Opposite: Observers watching from the relative safety of Nazaré's iconic red lighthouse on the head of the peninsula speak of the almighty thundering, shaking and deafening boom and crash as the mega-waves hit the shore. It is itself an experience to behold.

Saut-d'Eau

A MERGING OF HOLY WATER AND VODOU MAGIC

- ✳ Haiti
- ✝ Vodou
- ⛪ 1849
- 👥 10,000
- 📅 14–16 July
- 📍 50 hectares (123.5 acres)

18°49'0" N 72°12'0" W

Travel 96 kilometres (60 miles) north of the Haiti's capital, Port au Prince, and you'll find Saut-d'Eau, the holiest of homes for the country's natives. This mystical waterfall – or "water jump" – captures the spirit of the Vodou religion, and it is a profound annual pilgrimage for thousands of Vodouisants.

On 16 July 1849, the Virgin Mary apparently appeared on a palm tree near a 30-metre (100-ft) waterfall in the Mirebalais arrondissement, in the Centre department of the island of Haiti. After Mary's apparition, the water and the surrounding grove became known far and wide as a sacred site that could cure the sick and help the needy. Today, thousands of Vodou pilgrims – Vodouisants – as well as spiritual tourists, travel to the waterfall every year to what is now revered as the "Miraculous Virgin of Saut d'Eau". Before the arrival of the Virgin Mary, the waterfall was already a geological curiosity and place of interest as it is believed that it sprang to life after a large earthquake hit the region on 7 May 1842. Within a few years of the sighting of the Virgin Mary, the site had been conflated with her Vodou counterpart, Erzulie Danto, a spirit in Haitian Vodou, an angel that represents the divinity of motherhood that is often depicted as the Black Madonna. This religious "syncretism" – the blending of two or more belief systems into a new religion – is a central feature of Vodou, where there is a deep-held desire to install native rituals and traditions with that of colonial beliefs.

The scores of thousands of sick and impoverished, as well as those simply seeking a spiritual retreat, come to bathe in the waterfall in a purification ritual that is known as a "luck bath", and is similar to baptism. Over the course of what is now an established three-day festival, Vodouisants swim and dive unclothed in the plunging waterfall and its waters, and pray and perform spiritual rites with an Ougan (Vodou priest). This latter is there to banish evil spirits and invite the protection and virtues of Erzulie Danto and the Virgin Mary. After the body, mind and spirit of the devoted have all been cleansed, the pilgrims go back on their way dressed in clean clothes. They have been rebirthed and imbued with a fresh sense of good luck and prosperous health – spiritually and economically – for the rest of the year. The well-established religion of Haitian Vodou is a unique mix of African religious practices and Christianity. It is a monotheistic religion and features Bondye, "the good god", as the central figurehead. An estimated 50 to 80 per cent of Haitians indulge in Vodou rituals, and there are believed to be a number as high as approximately 60 million Vodou followers in the world. It is spelled differently from the word 'voodoo' in order to distinguish itself from the practices of American voodoo, which is still actively practised in and around the city of New Orleans, Louisiana, in the United States.

Opposite: Vodou rituals take place during the pilgrimage weekend, including animal sacrifice, the drawing of symbols, and Vodou dolls (not the pin variety), which are totems of worship to honour the Virgin Mary.

Snæfellsjökull

A MAJESTIC LANDMARK AT THE MEETING OF LAVA AND ICE

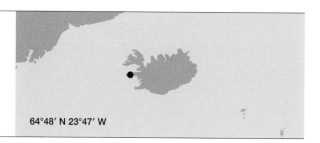

⊛ Iceland

✝ Natural/Pre-Christian

🏛 900 CE

👥 2 million

📅 June–August

🗺 170 km² (65 sq. mi.) (park)

64°48′ N 23°47′ W

Towering 1,446 metres (4,744 ft) above the local landscape, western Iceland's Snæfellsjökull glacier is an all-natural attraction of unquestionable spiritual strength, glowing with mysticism, energy and elegance, and considered by many as one of the planet's most powerful centres of spiritual energy.

Pronounced 'snae-fell-syo-skul', and translated into English as "snow-fell glacier", Snæfellsjökull is a 700,000-year-old glacier-capped stratovolcano that – as many others in Iceland – is still considered active. It gives a supremely supernatural aura as it rises atop the tip of a peninsula scattered with dramatic lava-sculpted mountains and shore-lined cliffs. A sleeping giant for more than 1,750 years (the last eruption was in 250 CE), Snæfellsjökull is highly regarded as the icon of Iceland's touristic star power and, unsurprisingly, is often the main character in Icelandic sagas, folkloric tales and legends.

Locals believe that the volcano has a special spiritual energy, a source of mysticism and mystery. Around 1,000 years ago, Bárður – a half-troll, half-human giant – became the guardian spirit of Snæfellsjökull when he decided to leave his human life behind and become one with the mountain. According to the *Sagas* (the famous medieval Icelandic texts), Bárður is worshipped on the peninsula and only called upon when the land, and its people, need him. That ancient legend lives on to this very day, with many folk believing that the rock formations near Snæfellsjökull are trolls who were touched by the sunlight as the day rose, and became petrified.

Snæfellsjökull had its fantastic, otherworldly status confirmed in literature when the famous French author Jules Verne chose the volcano to be the entrance to the centre of the earth in his hugely influential, timeless novel *Journey to the Centre of the Earth*, in 1864. Snæfellsjökull certainly feels as if it could actually fulfil that role in real life – such is its dramatic geology and landscape, that ranges from the blue-hued glacier and moss-covered lava fields to caves, sea cliffs and black sand beaches.

The entirety of Snæfellsjökull is enclosed in the large Snæfellsjökull National Park, which covers pretty much all of the south-western tip of the peninsula that houses the volcano. A pleasant day trip from the island's capital Reykjavik, a great many visitors come to see the sites, particularly in the summer. Walking to the summit is a beautiful, challenging climb and the variety of landscapes can be stunning, as it ranges from ocean views to rock faces. In winter there is obviously less diversity and a different sort of challenge emerges. However, the dulled silence that the snow can bring on a short winter's day can, in its own way, be as inspiring and moving as the blue sky and sun.

To this day, the volcano continues to inspire many international authors, poets, artists and legends, hoping to grow closer to its power. It is visited all year round, but is most spectacular in the winter.

Opposite: Snæfellsjökull is now part of the Snæfellsjökull National Park, one of the three national parks in Iceland, and established in 2001.

Sossusvlei

A SACRED ASSEMBLY OF SAND, SEA AND SPIRITUALITY

⊛ Namibia

† Natural

🏛 1400 CE

👥 1 million

📅 July–October

🗺 5 hectares (12 acres)

24.7274° S, 15.3424° E

The Namib Desert is the oldest, driest and most inhospitable desert in the world, with an origin dating back more than 55 million years. Its isolation imbues it with many spiritual mysteries that are still waiting to be solved.

This famous sea of silica stretches across Namibia's entire southeast Atlantic coast. In the local Nama language, *Sossus* means "place of no return", and it is, indeed, a place of curious contradictions: both a location where life is near-impossible to sustain and yet it is teeming; a space with no immediate spiritual compass, and yet it is seemingly enveloped entirely by it; it is calm but wild.

The first point of fascination for visitors to this sacred landscape is the rolling, red sand dunes – probably the entire region's most popular tourist attraction. These well-known sand dunes are famed for their smooth and ever-changing peaks that sculpt the horizon as far as the eye can see, and even glow in a surreal spectrum – the colours ranging from deep orange and yellow hues to bright reds and pinks. The colour of the dunes is due to the oxidation of the huge concentrations of iron in the sand.

The dunes in this area are also some of the highest in the world. Many are greater than 200 metres (655 ft) in height. For example, Dune 7 – or Big Daddy, as it is affectionately known by locals – soars more than 400 metres (1,300 ft) into the sky, and is famed far and wide as the tallest sand dune in the world. From its zenith, visitors are said to be able witness a spectacular panorama – especially at the key times of sunset and sunrise – a view that offers an otherworldly sense of spiritual connection with the earth as the horizon seemingly bursts into flames that gleam bright in multiple shades of yellow, red and green. Almost as famous, and another sure place on the visiting list, is the Deadvlei ("Dead Marsh"): a white clay pan that was formed more than 1,000 years ago when the Tsauchab River flooded after heavy rainfall. This led to the creation of shallow pools of water, which in turn evaporated in the super-high heat that followed. In these puddles, acacia trees (known locally as camelthorn) began to grow. Within two centuries the regular heavy rain changed to severe drought, which meant that the trees were unable to decompose, and were left standing still for eternity. They make up a sight that is as bizarre as it is bewitching.

There are even petrified sand dunes that have formed over the years – this truly is an area of life and death, with even the sands beyond exception. And with an average high temperature of 34.5°C (94.1°F) that drops to an average low of 7.9°F (46.2°F), the desert is as inhospitable as you would imagine. But the silence of the desert, with its strange, bewitching colour schemes, makes this a supremely spiritual, almost magical place to visit.

Opposite: Sossusvlei is also famed for the presence of the strange and surreal "Fairy Circles". These large rings in the sand, which disappear and return over time, have no known origin. The local Himba and Herero people believe they are the footprints left by their supreme creator god, Mukuru.

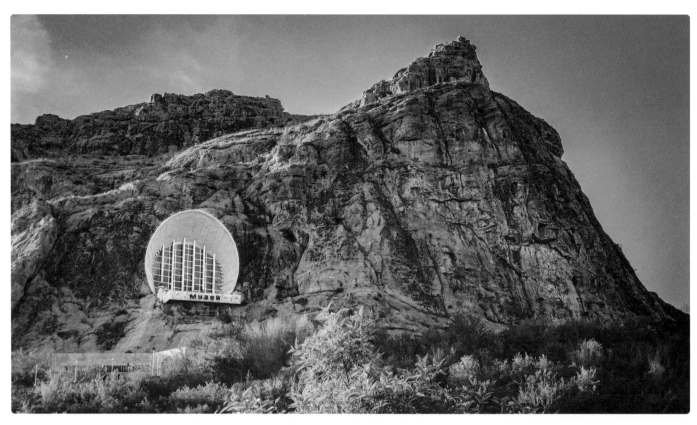

Sulaiman-Too

THE SILK ROAD'S SACRED STONE TOWER

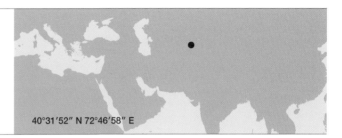

- ⊛ Kyrgyzstan
- ✝ Islam
- 🏛 500 CE
- 👥 2,000
- 📅 May/September
- ⊗ 1.12 km² (0.43 sq. mi.)

40°31'52" N 72°46'58" E

Sticking up like a spiritual sore thumb from the long, flat plains and fertile soils of the once-famous Fergana Valley in Kyrgyzstan is Sulaiman-Too, a once-blessed beacon of light for weary travellers and a sacred mountain to many, bestowed with amazing legends of Islam.

Sulaiman-Too Mountain and the area around it has been a popular place of worship for more than 1,500 years. It even predates the origins of Islam and has several fascinating links to Zoroastrianism, the world's oldest organized faith and what is acknowledged as precursor to many of today's world religions.

A geological and geographical curiosity, the site is a mound of lumpy limestone, weathered and worn with carved crevices, canopies and caves, and sits at a vital crossroads along the historic Central Asian Silk Road system, where it acted as lighthouse, alerting travellers that they had at last reached the important trading town of Osh.

The mountain – pointing 175 metres (575 ft) skywards – was described 1,000 years ago by the Greek geographer and mathematician Ptolemy, in his world-first world map *Geographica*, as the "stone tower that marked the midpoint on the Silk Road", the most important landmark on this legendary route of antiquity.

A millennia before this mapping, however, the mountain was employed as a canvas for the carving of petroglyphs: suns, labyrinths and hunting weapons, the common cave illustration inspirations for followers of Mithra, the Zoroastrian sun god, also worshipped by the Greek and Romans at one time.

Sulaiman-Too offered early disciples of Zoroastria a spiritual home as its five peaks neatly resembled – or took inspiration from – the mountain described in the *Avesta*, the religious texts of the Zoroastrian faith, whereby a single mountain with a peak dominating four others, standing in the virtual centre of a vast river valley symbolized the centre of the universe. It is the same quincunx shape that represents the mythical Mount Meru in Buddhist and Hindu doctrine, seen in many other spiritual places around Asia and the Far East.

Sulaiman-Too – the name means "the throne of Solomon" – remains a place of huge importance for Muslims. The stone tower takes its name from Solomon, the son of David, King of Israel, and a prophet in the Quran, who, according to legend, lived on the mountain around 1000 BCE. Today, a shrine supposedly marks his grave. It is believed that females who visit the shrine (and crawl across a holy rock) will give birth to healthy children. This is just one of the many traditional birth rituals that take place inside the mountain's "cave wombs", as they are known. Every year, Muslim pilgrims visit the mountain to lean, slide down, touch and rub smooth various rocks deemed holy in the hope of receiving healing for fertility issues and enhancing vitality.

Opposite above: A Soviet-era building, now a museum, was constructed in one of the large caves of the mountain.
Opposite below: In 2009, the mountain was honoured by UNESCO for its exceptional spiritual landscape that reflects both pre-Islamic and Islamic beliefs.

Table Mountain

A FLAT-TOPPED PLATFORM WITH THE BEST VIEW TO WATCH THE WORLD GO BY

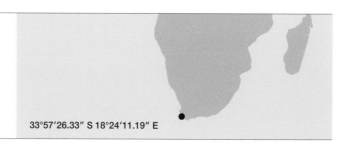

✳ South Africa

✝ Natural

🏛 1100 CE

👤 4.2 million

📅 All year round

⛰ 1,084 m (3,558 ft) (height)

33°57′26.33″ S 18°24′11.19″ E

Older than the Andes, the Alps, the Rocky Mountains and the Himalayas, Table Mountain has witnessed world evolution for more than 250 million years, making it one of the world's oldest peaks. Time enough to imbue it with many sacred myths and legends...

Table Mountain has the rare distinction of being a mountain with no discernible peak – just a massive sunroof.

In 1998, former South African President Nelson Mandela proclaimed Table Mountain "a gift to the earth". It's an understatement, to say the least. Today, Table Mountain is the nation's most photographed natural monument and, from its flat-topped vantage point, a landmark where visitors of antiquity watched the old world of the east transform into the new world of the west, as divided by the Cape of Good Hope, the most southern point of the African continent. It is now part of the Table Mountain National Park, which is protected under UNESCO as a World Heritage Site since 1998.

Table Mountain and the surrounding area has long been considered a meeting point of historical and spiritual origins. The Khoisan, the very first inhabitants of South Africa and whose descendants make up a great deal of South Africa's black population today, had a special name for the mountain: *Hoerikwaggo*. It means "Mountain of the Sea". That was, of course, for its front-row view over the precise spot where the Atlantic and Indian oceans collide. That fact alone is quite possibly worthy of Table Mountain's admission into the pantheon of rock gods.

One of the most enduring spiritual myths attached to the mountain's name is the "The Watcher of the South", a legend told by the Xhosa people about their supreme creation gods,

Qamata, and the son of the sun god, Thixo, and the earth goddess, Jobela. As Qamata began creating land he was forced into battle with the dragon, Nkanyamba, the sea god. A fight ensued, leading to Jobela to protect her son by creating stone giants to defend the four corners of the world from the dragon. Once Qamata defeated Nkanyamba and enough land had formed on the earth, the giants she had created died and turned into stone, to watch over the four points of the earth for ever more. The biggest and strongest of these giants was named *Umlindi Wemingizimu*, the Watcher of the South, or as it is referred to today, Table Mountain.

Another famous meeting occurs on the famous flat top of the mountain, when it is often covered by orographic clouds, giving the impression the mountain is shrouded in a "tablecloth" of cloud. This distinct cloud formation is created when wind travels up the mountain slopes and condenses on contact with the cooler summit air.

These days the mountain's national park is a popular destination for visitors and tourists, local and from further afield. There is a cableway up the mountain if the ascent is deemed to be too much – or for a breathtaking view in the air.

Opposite: More than 70 per cent of the 1, 470 species of flower found on the summit of Table Mountain – the richest floral kingdom on earth – are unique to that spot.

Uluru

THE ULTIMATE ICON OF AUSTRALIA'S INDIGENOUS CULTURE AND ITS SPIRITUAL CENTRE

✳ Australia

† Aboriginal

🏛 30,000 years

👥 250,000

📅 May–September

🗺 1,326 km² (512 sq. mi.) (park)

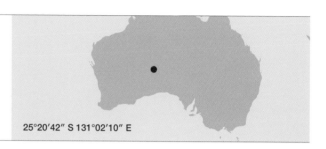

25°20'42" S 131°02'10" E

For the Anangu people, a collection of local but distinct Aboriginal tribes, Uluru is much more than a monolithic sandstone emerging from the earth. It is a living, breathing, sacred monument, formed by ancestral beings during the Dreaming.

At the heart of Australia is where Uluru lies, both spiritually and geographically. And confusingly, the site where Uluru emerges from the earth can also be described as being in the southern part of the Northern Territory in the Western Desert.

The entire area is, unarguably, the most important indigenous site in the country. Anangu tribes have roamed around the 60-million-year-old Uluru for 60,000 of those years. They count themselves as one of the oldest continuous cultures in the world and have become one with the landmark, weaving its protrusive nature, stature and iridescent red glow into their traditional belief system and divine storytelling, known as the Dreaming.

According to the ancient legends that are still recounted by the Anangu, Uluru was formed by a race of ancestral beings millions of years ago, during the creation of the earth, and is now used as a resting place: still, but alive. Today, the Anangu hold ceremonies in caves and fissures that line the base of the "Great Pebble" – the English translation of *Uluru* – and recount tales of the religious philosophy that guides their way of life, the *Tjukurpa* (pronounced "chook-orr-pa"). Much relates to the beginning of time when the land, the rock and the people were shaped and created by their ancestor spirits. The *Tjukurpa* are far from simple, moralistic fairy tales: they are rich and complex creation stories that detail the structure of the universe and all life within it, and are passed down through generations. Many of the stories contain practical

lessons about the land and how to survive in it. It is said that Uluru was, indeed, created by these spirits to teach the Anangu about how the land on this precious earth is sacred – and how it is to be respected as a living creature. As a result of this spiritual significance, Uluru is – since 2017 – finally forbidden to be climbed by tourists. Prior to this date, vast numbers of visitors would ignore the many polite signs that explained the spiritual significance of the site to the indigenous population, and clamber up it, leaving tracks and rubbish.

Towering 348 metres (1,141 ft) above its surrounding flat sand plains and woodland, Uluru is taller than the Eiffel Tower in Paris and almost as high as the Empire State Building in New York. This discounts the fact that most of Uluru's colossal mass is beneath the surface and extends at least another 2.5 kilometres (1.5 miles) underground.

Uluru reclaimed its original aboriginal name in 2002 from Ayers Rock, the name given to the monolith when explorer William Gosse saw it and named it after his Chief Secretary of South Australia, Sir Henry Ayers, in 1873.

Opposite: Spiritual seekers who arrive at sunset are gifted with Uluru's dramatic shift of colour, from various tones of red to violet to orange. Visitors can walk around the site but are not permitted to mount the stone – a sign of disrespect towards the place and those who venerate it.

CHAPTER 5

Centres of Enlightenment

The religions that are dominant in southeast Asia, Shinto and Buddhism for example, are perhaps closer to philosophies than formal religions. A oneness with various elements is a common theme, with spirit, nature and family prominent. Although different from Christian-based religions, shrines and temples have been constructed for centuries, and are some of the most impressive buildings in that part of the world.

Boudhanath

A SPHERICAL STUPA THAT ENSHRINES THE REMAINS OF AN ANCIENT BUDDHA

- Nepal
- Buddhist
- 600 CE
- 1.9 million
- October/November
- 36 m (118 ft) (height)

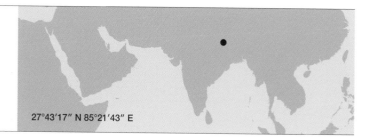

27°43'17" N 85°21'43" E

As wide as Myanmar's Schwegadon Pagoda (*see* page 198) is tall (100 metres/300 ft), Nepal's Boudhanath is the world's largest spherical stupa. Seen from above, this monument to Buddha is a massive mandala as well, pointing all the way to the mystical Mount Meru.

For more than 1,500 years after its establishment, and shortly after the death of the first Buddha, Boudhanath was revered by another name: Khasti Mahachaitya, or "the stupa of a million dew drops". According to Nepalese legend, the stupa was built in its location because it is the precise spot where the head of King Vikramaditya – the ruler at the time and subject of various traditional stories of the region – landed after he was executed by his own son. The king had offered himself as a human sacrifice to the gods in the hope that rain would fall and the 12-year-long drought would end. After the beheading, the prince was so horrified by his actions that he travelled to a nearby temple and spent the next few years of his life praying for forgiveness to Tara, the Buddhist goddess of mercy and compassion. Eventually, the goddess heard his prayer and guided the prince to build a temple from dew drops to wash away his sin. And so Khasti Mahachaitya was built and it has been Nepal's beacon of light ever since. However, it did change its name...

As with many of the world's most important spiritual centres, the shape of the structure is just as important as the site itself. For example, the pyramids in Ancient Egypt represent the sun's rays. Pagodas and stupas in Asia are shaped to symbolize the iconic meditation pose of the Buddha, which is wide at the base before reaching to a tall peak. As Buddhists believe that the accumulation of wealth should lead to charity and good deeds, it is quite common to find Buddhist stupas covered in gold. The temple at Boudhanath is no exception and is covered with what is estimated to be 30 kilograms (66 lb) of it, with an approximate value of US$1.5 million. And underneath the gleaming golden spire lie hidden the remains – so legend says – of Kassapa Buddha, one of the five central Buddhas (each one representing a different aspect of consciousness).

The stupa's multi-tiered profile – from square base to white dome to golden tip – is centred on a five-layered mandala, with each ascending level representing the journey towards Mount Meru. At the top of the stupa, above the eyes of Buddha, is a golden pyramid made of 13 steps, decreasing in diameter as they reach the peak. This stairway up represents "Bodhi", the 13 steps Buddhists must complete to obtain enlightenment.

Tethered to ropes that attach to the golden peak are thousands of colourful prayer flags. Each flag represents a prayer, or a mantra. With each gust of breeze, the prayer takes flight from the flag to ascend heavenwards where, hopefully, it will be seen by the Gods.

Opposite: Viewed from above, the distinctive shape of the stupa and compound is clear. The mandala shape is important in Buddhism, representing a guiding principle or aspect of wisdom. This huge one points the way to Mount Meru.

Chiu Gompa Monastery

A HILLTOP TOMB WITH A SPARROW'S VIEW OF SACRED MOUNT KAILASH

⊛ Tibet

✝ Multifaith

🏛 Circa 750 CE

🁢 470,000

🗓 May–October

📍 4,590 m (15,059 ft) (elevation)

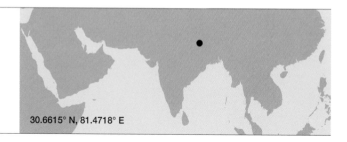

30.6615° N, 81.4718° E

In Tibet, a *gompa* is different from a typical monastery. It must be in a "remote place" (the precise translation) as it is a sacred space Buddhists go to meditate and immerse their mind, body and soul in their spiritual monastic teachings.

In Western Tibet, where it is cold, rugged and windy all year round, Chiu Gompa is protected from up on high by the ever-watchful nearby eye of Mount Kailash in the north. That is Tibet's most sacred mountain, as well as a fantastic lookout spot to see the sacred shores of Lake Manasarovar, the highest and holiest freshwater body in the world. For people of the Hindu faith, the lake is a personification of purity, and anyone who drinks its water will live in peace with Lord Shiva after their death, cleansed of all sins from the act of imbibing. According to followers of the Hindu religion, the lake was first created in the mind of Lord Brahma after which it was manifested on the earth. In Sanskrit, Manasarovar marries together the English words for "mind" and "lake" and Brahma believed it to the perfect spot for religious rituals.

Back to the mountain: carved into the cliff's edge of the craggy red-hued Sangtok Pelri mountain at 4,590 metres (15,059 ft) of oxygen-thinning altitude, the monastery takes its name from the legend of Padmasambhava, also known as Guru Rinpoche. He was a fully enlightened being, who, according to Buddhist legend, was guided to this spot by a sparrow (*Chiu* meaning "sparrow" in the Tibetan language) for the final seven days of his life, where he meditated. And before he died, he left his mark on the world with a footprint set in stone, which the monastery was then built around. Today, the footprint is a super-spiritual point of pilgrimage for the local Jain and Bön religions, as well as being highly revered by Buddhists.

On a visit to the monastery, pilgrims may also bathe in the hot springs that are located not far behind. In fact, so basic are the facilities in some of the guesthouses by the nearby lake, that the springs take the place of showers. This cleanliness is encouraged by all.

Although not the largest, the most remote, the highest or any single record-holder, the Temple of Chiu Gompa is beautiful, serene, simple and deeply spiritual. In a world where many places of worship have become utterly overcrowded, enormously busy and nothing more than a tick-off point for global travellers and tourists, it is refreshing to visit a place that goes back to the basics of spirituality: it's all about the feeling. And the feeling you get when observing the sky when meaningful temple, lake and mountain are all lit up together at dawn or dusk is like nothing that will be experienced anywhere on earth.

Opposite: Many Tibetan pilgrims visit this sacred area to complete two-pilgrim rituals, known as *Kora*. First, they circumnavigate Lake Manarsarovar, then visit the monastery and for the second one, they circumnavigate holy Mount Kailash, a 51-kilometre (32-mile) round trip. Each revolution of the celestial bodies is one step closer to nirvana.

Golden Temple of Amritsar

THE WORLD'S MOST GOLDEN *GURDWARA* FLOATS ON A SCARED POOL

- ✳ India
- ✝ Sikh
- 🏛 1581
- 👤 18.5 million
- 📅 Oct–Nov/Feb–March
- 📍 6.2 m² (67 sq. ft)

31°37'12" N 74°52'35" E

Known as the world's most visited religious place, the Golden Temple of Amritsar is known to Sikhs all over the world as Harimandir Sahib – the House of God.

Today, there are approximately 30 million Sikhs worldwide, making Sikhism the world's fifth-largest major religion, but also the youngest, as it originated in the 15th century. Sikhs follow the teachings of ten gurus or special religious leaders. They believe in one god and that all people are equal. For every Sikh on earth, the Golden Temple is their spiritual home.

There are many striking features about this place of worship, or *gurdwara*, located in the holy city of Amritsar, in the Punjab province, that distinguishes itself from religious structures of other world religions. Firstly, ever since 1830, its 6.2-metre-(67-ft)-square, two-story marble foundation holds up a shining golden dome, lined with more than 400 kg (881 lb) of gold leaf – its purpose to shine for bright for all Sikhs and reflect the temple's grandeur and importance.

Next, the temple floats on a pool of man-made water, known as the Amrit Sarovar, or Pool of Nectar of Immortality. The pool has become so sacred they named the city after it. Before giving prayer, Sikh pilgrims bathe in the holy water and believe that their bodies become possessed with good spirits. According to Sikh scripture, a dip in the holy pool can cure ill health, too.

The foundation stone of marble was laid more than 500 years ago, in 1581, and it took eight years to complete. It was one of the original Sikh *gurdwaras*, but not the first. That one was built in Kartarpur, on the banks of Ravi River, in 1521. The original

temple, built by Arjan, the fifth Sikh guru – one of the first Sikhs to be martyred and the compiler of Sikh wisdom in the holy book, *Guru Granth Sahib* – believed that the Golden Temple must treat all humans as equals in accordance with Sikh beliefs. So he placed the temple below street level so that everyone was humbled stepping down into the main temple room.

The temple is, of course, more than just a place of worship to the Sikh god, Ik Onkar. It is where several rites from the Sikh scripture are read out every day. Sikhs treat the rites and the scripture of the *Guru Granth Sahib* as if a living person, and treat it with the utmost reverence.

According to Sikh legend, one of the most iconic martyrs, Baba Deep Singh, vowed to take his last breath inside the temple. In 1757, when the holy city was under invasion by the Afghan army led by Jahan Khan, Baba Deep Singh fought off this "battle of 5,000 men" bravely. During the battle, his head was cut off by a sword. However, Singh held his head high with one hand and continued to fight off enemies until he reached the temple – and promptly died on its floor.

Opposite: The world's largest free kitchen, or *langar sewa*, operates outside the entrance of the Golden Temple. It serves more than 50,000 vegetarian meals every day to anyone who arrives, regardless of race or religion.

Haedong Yonggungsa Temple

A VISION-INSPIRED SEASIDE SPIRITUAL CENTRE

- ✴ South Korea
- ✝ Buddhist
- ⬛ 1376
- 👥 Unknown
- 📅 March/April
- 📍 36 m (118 ft) (height)

27°43'17" N 85°21'43" E

In South Korea's bustling second city, Busan, this beautiful water temple, set into cliff's edge beside the sea, is the most beloved spiritual icon of the nation and a popular pilgrimage for Buddhists and plenty of other spiritual travellers. Thank Buddha we're here – at Haedong Yonggungsa Temple.

The only ocean-facing Buddhist temple in the whole of South Korea (most of the country's temples are located up in the mountains), Haedong Yonggungsa Temple, an eight-storey pagoda, is immediately discernible as a rare place of worship. Its history dates back more than 700 years and it is cherished for its mythical creation stories as well as its location and temple. Local legend tells a tale of the day when a divine sea god named Yongsin appeared to the Buddhist teacher Naong Hyegeun, who was an advisor to the king during the Goryeo dynasty (918–1392), and a figure responsible for installing Buddhism in South Korea. In a dream, the sea god instructed Naong to build a temple where the mountain meets the sea – the teacher understanding that to mean there at Haedong Yonggungsa, where the temple stands today. Yongsin further told that if Buddhists came to pray on that spot, that they would find happiness without hardship.

Naong did as the sea god told and travelled to Haedong Yonggungsa, believing it to be place Yongsin intended and built his temple, a place in perfect harmony with nature. Following completion of the temple in 1376, Naong honoured the goddess of mercy, Guan Yin, a deity in Buddhist teachings, with its first name, Bomun. However, some six centuries later,

in 1974, Jeong-am, the temple's then head monk, had a vision during his *jeong-geon kido*, or 100 days of non-stop prayer. The head monk's vision was of the goddess of mercy. In it, she was cloaked in a white gown and riding a beam of light on the back of a dragon. After he gained consciousness, Jeong-am renamed the temple Haedong Yonggungsa – the Korean Dragon Palace Temple and the legend was born.

The entrance to the pagoda is guarded by four stone lions. They are there to greet pilgrims, and they symbolize joy, anger, sadness and happiness. Passing them, with the gentle sound of the ocean in the background, visitors mount the 108 steps up through a pine grove, crossing a bridge, in order to reach the upper heights of the temple and the other buildings and monuments in the complex. Inside one of the shrines is a large golden Buddha statue that surveys the ocean, day and night.

Opposite: The entire cliff-side complex is visible (above), with the distinctive and colourful pagoda-style temple. (Below), statues of each animal from the Chinese zodiac line the path. They are reputed to block the invasion of evil spirits.

Khamar Monastery

DEVOTION TO THE DIVINE IN THE DESERT

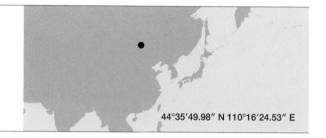

⊛ Mongolia

✝ Tibetan Buddhist

🏛 1820

👥 100,000

📅 March–August

⚲ 25 hectares (61 acres)

44°35'49.98" N 110°16'24.53" E

At the foot of one of the sacred mountains in Mongolia, and in the old stomping grounds of the 13th-century ruler Genghis Khan and his Mongol nation, is where you'll discover Khamariin Khid, or Khamar Monastery, glowing from the golden sand of the Gobi's spiritual power.

Built in 1821 on a site that was chosen for its proximity to the Gobi Desert, a region believed by Tibetan Buddhists in Mongolia (approximately 50 per cent of the population) to be the centre of the world's spiritual energy, this monastery is truly remote. But every day, hundreds of Buddhist pilgrims visit the monastery at sunrise to soak in the spiritual energy given to the world from the sun to celebrate a new day. Also, as part of a ritual of rebirth, they throw rice on many of the monastery's many monuments. This is in honour of the Buddha and his 12-step teachings to self-enlightenment.

This sacred monastery and its collection of meditation caves, was, according to legend, founded by a 17-year-old Mongolian monk named Dulduityn Danzanravjaa. He was a beloved Buddhist lama (spiritual leader), scholar and social reformer, and was further believed to be the fifth incarnation of the Gobi Noyon Hutagt, a prominent family in the lineage of Tibetan Buddhism. Today, locals praise Danzanravjaa as a living god, despite his earthly passing in 1856. Sometimes referred to as "the Terrible Noble Saint of the Gobi", Danzanravjaa was a fierce critic of the traditional and oppressive Mongolian society of his era. As a reformer, he actively supported education for all, respected gender equality and founded the monastery on the edge of the desert with the principles of an enlightened society at the forefront of his wishes.

At the centre of the small complex is *Shambala*, a word which derives from Sanskrit texts to mean "place of tranquillity". Here, 108 stupas surround 80 small shrine-like temples, the most prominent of which sports a large pair of blue eyes that stare at passers-by from the hot desert sands. At its peak, the original monastery housed more than 5,000 monks, who reportedly cut themselves off from the world in one of the meditation caves for 108 days in the hope of nirvana knocking on their door. (The number 108 is sacred in Tibetan Buddhism for it correlates with the 108 volumes of sacred texts described as the *Word of the Buddha* as well as the 108 temptations each Buddhist must face on the road to nirvana).

In 1937, the first monastery was razed to the ground in a violent act carried out by pro-Stalinist supporters and part of the Stalinist purges that blighted the country between 1937 and 1939. As well as destruction of many of the buildings, a number of the monastery's lamas were slaughtered. The monastery that stands today was built in 1990, carefully following the architecture design of the original.

Opposite: Small shrines and stupas cover the landscape of the temple complex, which houses a number of larger buildings and a main, central stupa. Fiery sunsets make the sky seem alive.

Maya Devi Temple

THE BIRTHPLACE AND CHILDHOOD HOME OF THE ENLIGHTENED ONE

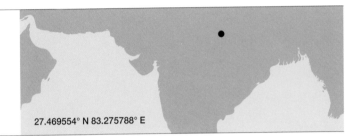

- ✳ Nepal
- ✝ Buddhist
- 🏛 623 BCE
- 👥 1.1 million
- 📷 April-May
- 🗺 776 hectares (1,917 acres)

27.469554° N 83.275788° E

In India and Nepal there are many incredible spiritual sites that celebrate the life and death of the Awoken One, Gautama Buddha. He grew enlightened in Bodh Gaya, gave his first sermon in Sarnath and died in Kushinagar. However, it is here, inside the Maya Devi Temple, some 2,500 years ago, that the Buddha was born.

He was to spend his childhood in the grounds of the "lovely" place of Lumbini (its translation in Sanskrit). And it is here where the man who would become known throughout the world and for thousands of years as Buddha first saw the beauty of this world – and the suffering within.

At the holy heart of the UNESCO-protected pilgrimage site of Lumbini resides the ancient Maya Devi Temple. Here Queen Māyā of Shakya gave birth to her son, Prince Siddhartha Gautama in (or around) 623 BCE. Before his untimely death (from food poisoning) the Lord Buddha spoke highly of his childhood home, Lumbini: "This place is where the Tathagata [the enlightened one] was born, this is a place which should be visited and seen by a person having faith, devotion and mindfulness which would cause the awareness and apprehensive nature of impermanence."

According to Buddhist teachings, Queen Maya died seven days after the birth of her son, leaving the prince to be raised by his maternal aunt, Mahapajapati Gotami. Queen Maya's spirit, however, on occasion would appear in Lumbini to speak with her son and offer sage advice. It was her counsel that encouraged humans to turn away from the never-ending demand of desire and follow a life of quiet contemplation.

Opposite Maya Devi Temple is a sacred pool, known as Puskarni, and it is still said to be a place of exceptional calm.

And rightfully so, for it is here that Maya Devi bathed before giving birth to the Buddha. In December 1896, archaeological remains from the 3rd century BCE were found – the Asoka Pillar – along with a famous inscription detailing Lumbini to be the birthplace of the Buddha. This was the first physical evidence of the Buddhist faith. The inscriptions on each side of the pillar was proof that King Asoka, who ruled the Indian subcontinent 200 years after Buddha's lifetime, wanted Buddhism to spread rapidly throughout his kingdom and beyond.

In 249 BCE, Asoka embarked on a royal pilgrimage to Lumbini and left behind some markers of its sacred greatness. Several of these "Ashokan pillars" can be found in Buddhist spiritual sites around India, in places pivotal to the life of the Buddha. They now act as markers for pilgrimages. Over the past 2,000 years, these monolithic stone pillars, which weigh about 50 tonnes (49 tons) each, symbolized the Axis Mundi – the axis upon which Buddhists believe the world spins.

Opposite: After the death of the Buddha, Lumbini was transformed into a place of pilgrimage and became one of the world's most important holy sites. Every day and night, Buddhist pilgrims from all over the world come to chant and meditate outside the Maya Devi Temple.

Palitana Temples

THE CITY OF A THOUSAND TEMPLES ON SACRED SHATRUNJAYA HILL

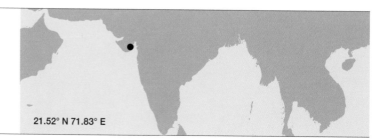

✴ India

✝ Jain

🏛 Circa 1100

👥 400,000

📅 November–February

⛰ 83 km² (32 sq. mi.)

21.52° N 71.83° E

In the Bhavnagar district of Gujarat, India, at the top of a breathtaking 3,750 stone steps – at an elevation of 2,221 metres (7,288 ft) – is an even more breathtaking view of an amazing mountain "city of a thousand temples" (in fact, it's more like 1,200) etched into the sacred Shatrunjaya Hill.

Pālītānā is home of the world's only mountain temple city, with both the mountains and the temple considered to be the most sacred pilgrimage place (or *tirtha*) to the world's 6 million Jains worldwide. They make up approximately 2 per cent of India's 1.4 billion population. However, most of the Jain community live here in the regions of Gujarat or Pālītānā.

This small city is closely associated with the multiple legends and creation myths of Jain. Ādinātha is the primeval lord of the Jain *tirthankaras*, a saviour figure and spiritual teacher. He is known to have meditated on Shatrunjaya Hill, where the Palitana Temples were later constructed more than 2,500 years ago. However, accordingly to Jainists, Ādinātha has been coming to Pālītānā, spiritually, for a lot longer.

In the traditional texts and beliefs of Jainsim, Ādinātha lived for more than 8 million years and is believed to have visited Satrunjaya Hill nearly 700 million times in his lifetime to meditate – more than any other Jain *tirtha*. For this reason, every devout Jain aspires to climb to the top of the mountain at least once in their lifetime in an effort to attain nirvana and to be closer to Ādinātha.

Jains believe in reincarnation, in a similar way to followers of the Hindu faith, but where the religions differ is that the Jaians seek to attain freedom by escaping the continuous cycle of birth, death and rebirth, so that their soul may live forever in a state of bliss. The way to do this, according to their teachings, is to reach enlightenment through non-violence and by not harming any another living beings, including plants and animals. It is for this reason that Pālītānā became the world's first vegetarian city. Here, in the shadow of the many temples, it is illegal to sell meat and even eggs are banned, too. And since 2014, no animal has been slaughtered either.

According to archaeological explorations and the architecture of this amazing place, it is thought that the first buildings were constructed around 1100. There has been a huge number of revisions, additions and rebuilds since then, of course (16 formal, official renovations are listed as having taken place on the site). However, since many temples before this time were built out of wood, it is likely that there were temples – or some form of place of organized worship – on the site before that date, and almost certain that people had been partaking in some form of religious ceremony for many years before that as well.

Opposite: The main temple, and the grandest in Pālītānā, is the Adinath Temple. Its exterior and interiors are completely covered with intricate and ornate architectural motifs, such as friezes of dragons. All of the larger temples are constructed out of white marble, to symbolize purity.

Paro Taktsang Monastery

AN ETHEREAL PLACE OF WORSHIP ON THE EDGE OF A MOUNTAIN

(✷) Bhutan

(✝) Tibetan Buddhist

(🏛) 1692

(👥) 55,000

(📅) March–May

(🗺) 2,848 km² (1,100 sq. mi.)

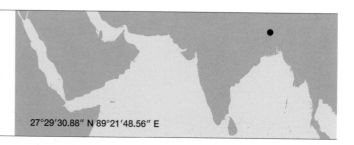

27°29'30.88" N 89°21'48.56" E

At the top of 800 stone slab stairs, after a five-hour, near-vertical 1,000-metre (3,280-ft)-hike, visitors will reach one of the world's most remote sacred places, and the envy of many other global tourist destinations: Paro Taktsang, a spellbinding spiritual nirvana unlike any other.

It might be light-headed delirium at simply reaching the top or pure spiritual enlightenment, but now that you're here at the foot of the "nest" don't look down – look up! When you do, you'll immediately see what all the fuss has been about. It is an awe-inspiring view, of a monastery in a mountain, as dizzying as it is dazzling, of a place founded solely to encourage the other side of the spirituality coin: serenity.

Nestled between China and India, micro-nation Bhutan's Paro Valley is full of emerald-green ravines and majestic mountain ranges largely untouched by humanity. At its spiritual heart resides Paro Taktsang, a ancient site of myth and mysticism, and now a sacred Himalayan Buddhist monastery temple complex carved into the cliff face. This perilously perched paradise is one of 13 historical "Tiger's Nest" caves throughout the area; these are destinations deemed worthy of a flying visit by the second reincarnation of the Buddha, Padmasambhava, who passed on the teachings of Tibetan Buddhism, known locally as Vajrayana.

Three centuries ago, this meditation cave was built by Gyalse Tenzin Rabgye, one of Bhutan's earliest rulers. Rabgye wanted to enshrine the spot into recorded history where, according to local Buddhist legend, he became Padmasmabhava. He had arrived at the top of the cliff by flying on the back of a tiger – hence the spot's English nickname, which is "The Tiger's Nest". And following his divine reincarnation, Rabgye anointed the spot as sacred and decided to build a monastery in its honour, and so introduced Bhutan to Buddhism.

This incredible white-with-gold-roof temple complex is a global icon of ornate Buddhist architecture; it houses four main temples that have a sole purpose of meditation and serenity. The temples are connected by stone staircases carved into the cliff's edge. The largest of the four prayer halls safeguards a large stone statue of Padmasambhava. It is that said that he meditated in this room for three years, three months, three weeks and three hours, never once leaving. Today, the handful of monks who reside here continue the tradition on their quest towards self-spiritual nirvana. In the Hall of the Thousand Buddhas, a large statue of a tiger, carved out of the rock, welcomes visitors and reminds them of the destination's spiritual history.

Paro Taktsang is often voted as one of the world's most popular adventure and hiking destinations. On the way up, explorers see thousands of colourful flags inscribed with prayers and mantras. As they flutter in the wind, the prayers are blown away into the world. It is believed by Tibetan Buddhists that any person touched by that breeze will receive the blessing of the flag.

Opposite: On 19 April 1998, the monastery was completely destroyed in a fire. It was rebuilt using the same local materials and technology as 300 years earlier.

Pashupatinath Temple

HOUSE OF WORSHIP ON THE ROOF OF THE WORLD

- ✳ Nepal
- ✝ Hindu
- 🏛 4380 BCE
- 👥 1.5 million
- 📅 March
- 🗺 6,000 m² (1.5 acres)

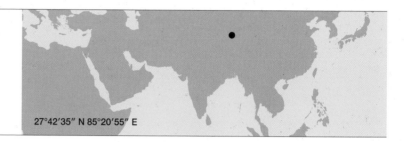

27°42'35" N 85°20'55" E

Nepal's capital, Kathmandu, is one of the oldest continuously inhabited cities in the world, established on divine foundations 2,000 years ago. Within its hallowed walls is Pashupatinath Temple – the holiest of holiest Hindu temples.

Nepal and Kathmandu are, unarguably, the world's greatest hotspots for spiritual enlightenment offered from two perspectives: natural and religious. Allowing a spiritual retreat for the soul among the heavens of the Himalayas, and the daunting height of Mount Everest, Nepal is rightly revered as "the roof of the world". It is a haven for mountain climbers and thrill seekers reaching their own peaks through physical and spiritual accomplishment. Far down in the valleys below, Kathmandu offers a divine destination for those seeking a religious encounter. Both can enrich the body, mind and soul.

Pashupatinath Temple complex is located along the banks of the Bagmati River – a transboundary that separates India and Nepal. The large complex is made up of a sprawling collection of temples and ashrams (a hermitage or monastery, most commonly used for Indian religions).

But the centrepiece is the Nepalese-style pagoda that is today considered to be one of the most important and secret holy pilgrimages sites for Hindu devotees all around the world, and it is a masterpiece of Hindu architecture: Pashupatinath Temple. Its creation and construction were designed to honour Pashupati, the first incarnation of Shiva, one of the Hindus' three primordial deities, and "lord of the animals", in human form. This temple was classified by UNESCO as a World Heritage Site in 1979. According to Hindus, Pashupatinath is the protector of the universe and the guardian of Nepali people.

The temple has deep spiritual significance and this is fully in evidence today, as it has been for hundreds of years. Every day on the bank of Bagmati River, outside the entrance of Pashupatinath Temple, an open-air cremation takes place. In it, the eldest son of the deceased shaves the head of the deceased and completes the cremation rites, offering the body up to the gods.

In the Hindu religion it is believed that Pashupatinath Temple is so sacred that if a person is lucky enough to be cremated on its premises they will be reincarnated as a human, regardless of any sins in their past lives. As a result, many elderly or unwell Hindus make a special pilgrimage to Pashupatinath from all over Nepal – and sometimes ever further afield – and spend the remaining few weeks of their lives in Pashupatinath Temple, awaiting their fate.

The temple itself is not open to non-Hindus, being so sacred to that religion. The distinctive, two-storied roof is made from copper but covered with gold, and sometimes it can be seen to glow in the afternoon light. Colourful sculptures, carvings and statues adorn the temple and everything is rich in meaning: a feast for the senses.

Opposite: Every 1 March, or new moon day, tens of thousands of Hindu pilgrims descend on Pashupatinath Temple for Nepal's primary pilgrimage festival, in keeping with traditions of their lunisolar calendar.

Shimogamo Shrine

THE OLDEST, MOST SACRED SHINTO TREASURE IN ALL OF KYOTO

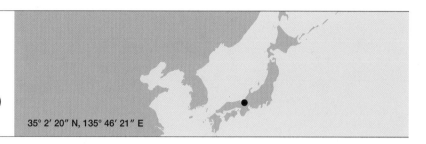

- ✳ Japan
- ✝ Shinto
- 🏛 678 CE
- 👥 500,000
- 📅 15 May
- 🗺 19,942 hectares (77 sq. mi.)

35° 2′ 20″ N, 135° 46′ 21″ E

The oldest Shinto shrine in Japan, Shimogamo is one of 17 awe-inspiring landmarks that celebrate the prestigious UNESCO-protected World Heritage Site Historic Monuments of Ancient Kyoto. This beautiful city is Japan's spiritual homeland and contains more sacred spaces than you can throw a *hashi* at, including this divine shrine…

Shimogamo Shrine is cherished by the nation's three million Shintoists. That is Japan's ancient, native religion, ever since its establishment in 678 CE, though its actual foundation no doubt dates back much earlier. In the country's former capital, Kyoto, there are many spiritual sites to grow wide-eyed at, but only three are Shinto, the remaining 13 belong to worshippers of the Buddhist faith.

Here, at Shimogamo, visitors will discover the most important and oldest shrine in Kyoto, alongside the younger Kamigamo Shrine, which is located downstream, alongside Japan's sacred primeval forest, Tadasu no Mori. Also to be found in the vicinity of the temple is Mitarashi Ike, a sacred pond. Let's dive in to the area and make a spiritual splash…

Located at the confluence of the Kamo River and the Takano River, the Shimogamo Shrine has always been revered as a protector guardian of Kyoto's ancient wonders. It was known as *Kamo-jinja* in Japanese and its task was mainly the protection of the city from evil spirits.

Known as the Ancestral Shrine (or *Kamo Mioya Jinja*), Shimogamo is the spiritual home to two of Shinto's main deities – the goddess Tamayori-hime, and her father, Kamo Taketsunomi. According to the historical texts of Japan's culture, the *Nihon Shoki* and *Kojiki*, Tamayori-hime was the mother of legendary Jimmu,

the first emperor of Japan, who began the process of uniting the nation in the 7th century. Feudalism was the only ruling system in Japan for many millennia and it took a long time to move on from it, painstakingly driven by men with vision.

For the 1,000 years that Kyoto served as Japan's capital city, a multitude of shrines were built to ensure the city's protection and prosperity. Surrounding Shimogamo is a sacred and mysterious, 12.4 hectares (30 acres) primal forest that is known as Tadasu no Mori ("the forest of purity"). It has been extremely well-preserved throughout the modernization of the city and contains more than 3,000 trees, including some ancient Japanese elm that are more than 600 years old.

Running its way through the forest is the Mitarashi River, which feeds the Mitarashi Ike, the famous pond in the grounds of Shimogamo that is said to purify bathers and drinkers of its spring water. Water is an essential element for Shinto followers, and so pilgrims who travel to Shimagamo cleanse themselves of impurity with water from the pond and the river.

Opposite: Shimogamo hosts Kyoto's biggest Shinto festival, the Aoi Matsuri. Every 15 May, a large procession of leaders and pilgrims walk to its sister shrine in Kamigamo dressed in traditional costume from the Heian period, when the shrines were built.

Shwedagon Pagoda

A SHINING STAR WORTH MORE THAN ITS WEIGHT IN GOLD

✳ Myanmar

✝ Buddhist

🏛 500 BCE

👥 500,000

📅 October and May

📍 46.3 hectares (114 acres)

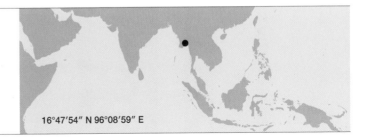

16°47'54" N 96°08'59" E

The Shwedagon Pagoda has lit up the Yangon skyline like a torch for almost 1,000 years – but it's much, much older than that. A spiritual Mecca for Myanmar's millions of Buddhists, and a top tick on the travel to-do lists for global explorers, it is, quite simply, as good as gold.

Myanmar's Shwedagon Pagoda is the world's oldest Buddhist stupa and was built more than 2,500 years ago. It's so ancient it dates to the actual lifetime of the Gautama Buddha, the first Buddha and founder of Buddhism. In that time, it has become Myanmar's most sacred Buddhist temple. Sitting pretty atop Singuttara Hill, the pagoda's elongated 112-metre (367-ft) tall, pure gold stupa can be seen from any spot in the city. As the esteemed English writer Rudyard Kipling once wrote of the pagoda, "a golden mystery upheaved itself on the horizon, a beautiful winking wonder that blazes in the sun, a shape neither Muslim dome nor Hindu temple-spire."

According to ancient Buddhist legend, Shwedagon is sacred because it houses an underground chamber with eight strands of hair from the head of Gautama Buddha, the fully enlightened being who is worshipped by half a billion Buddhists worldwide. The story goes that two merchant brothers, Tapussa and Bhallika, who, after meeting the Buddha, were given eight strands of his hair. The brothers offered the strands of hair to the then-ruler of Myanmar, King Okkalapa of Dagon. The king enshrined the hairs in a small stupa on the Singuttara Hill, which is the site of today's much larger, much more lavish, Shwedagon Pagoda.

For those wondering why the pagoda is covered head to toe in gold, it is due to a tradition that was started by Queen Shin Sawbu, one of the first Myanmar queens to rule southeast Asia in the 15th century. The queen famously donated her weight in gold to the pagoda as an offering in order to maintain the monument – and in so doing hoped to be rewarded in this life as well as in future incarnations. That was in accordance with her Buddhist beliefs and part of a ritual that powerful and wealthy Buddhist devotees, including monarchs and leaders from all over Asia, continued for centuries. Today, the central pagoda is plated with more than 20,000 gold bars: priceless.

The stupa's crown, known as the "umbrella", is covered with 5,500 diamonds, 2,300 rubies and 4,000 golden bells. At the very top of the umbrella, however, is the crown jewel – a 72-carat diamond, which is valued at US $3 billion. It is worth every cent.

There are four other pagodas that are very similar. One, in Napyidaw, Myanmar's capital city, is a full replica but a few inches smaller than the original. The others are in Indonesia (Lumbini Natural Park), India (the Global Vipassana Pagoda) and Myanmar (Tachileik Shwedagon Pagoda, near the border with Thailand and Laos).

Opposite: The golden stupa (above) gleaming as day turns to night. A powerful earthquake caused the main stupa to completely collapse in 1768, but a higher version was built some eight years later.

Wat Pho Temple

MEDICINE, EDUCATION AND SCIENCE COMBINE BEFORE A GIANT RECLINING BUDDHA

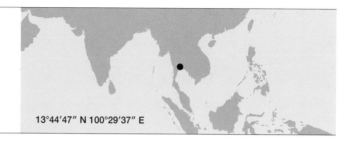

- ✳ Thailand
- ✝ Buddhist
- 🏛 1688
- 👥 1 million
- 📅 October/November
- 🗺 8 hectares (19.7 acres)

13°44'47" N 100°29'37" E

Stepping into Wat Pho Temple from the busy streets of the Thai capital Bangkok, it's not hard to see why this is such a revered place of worship. It delivers perfectly as a haven of peace in a built-up, teeming metropolis and is the perfect antidote to the teeming city streets.

The full, official name of this outstanding Buddhist temple is Wat Phracheatupon Vimonmungkraram – so it is possibly no surprise it is known globally as Wat Pho, which means "the temple of the reclining Buddha". That Buddha is, indeed, a wonder to behold and is one of the largest reclining Buddha statues in the world, measuring 46 metres (151 ft) long and 15 metres (49 ft) high. The statue is covered in gold and features mother-of-pearl decoration on its enormous feet, which are also decorated with 108 colourful scenes from the life of the Buddha.

The entire temple complex is vast and contains 99 pagodas, the highest number of any temple complexes in Thailand. Wat Pho is also the largest and oldest Buddhist temple in Thailand, with yet another claim to fame being that it is the spiritual home of Thai massage; you can get one on the temple grounds – particularly recommended after a long, hot day spent exploring the buildings and the grounds.

Built originally in the late 17th century, between 1688 and 1703, during the reign of King Phetracha, the first temple on the site of Wat Pho was evacuated around 100 years afterwards. War and a new king were the reasons for the abandonment and the temple fell into ruin. Late in the 18th century, however, King Rama I ordered the reconstruction. A number of images of the Buddha were salvaged from other notable and disused temples in the vicinity, including Ayutthaya (*see* page 58) and Sukhothai.

Wat Pho was always designed to be a place of eduction as well as a place of worship, and carved into marble and dotted around the complex are 1,360 inscriptions of fascinating written information on subjects such as medicine, Thai massage, history, health and Buddhist religious practices. This serves to further highlight the temple's establishment as a space for monks, worshippers and visitors alike: everyone has something to learn here, and all are welcome. It is for this reason that the temple has been known as "the nation's first public university".

Everywhere you turn on a visit to this endlessly fascinating place is a feast for the eyes, the intellect and the spirit: a wide range of architecture, intricately decorated temples, shiny statues, carefully carved beams and beautifully looked-after gardens make this a location for all forms of sustenance. And time seems to work in a different way here, too: an entire day can easily be swallowed up pacing the gardens, wondering at the beauty and, above all, learning new subjects, for example human anatomy, liberal sciences and the importance of spirituality in this busy, busy world.

Opposite: The ubosot (an ordination hall), is pictured bottom right. Above: the gold–copper alloy Buddha is a nine-tiered umbrella, which represents the authority of Thailand.

Yungang Grottoes

THE ZENITH OF BUDDHIST SPIRITUALITY, SET IN STONE

⁕ China

✝ Chinese Buddhist

🏛 465 CE

👥 200,000

📖 March–May

🗺 18,000 m² (193,750 sq. ft)

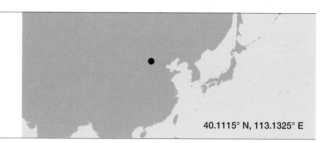

40.1115° N, 113.1325° E

Proving the point that not all masterpieces must be hung on a gallery wall, some, like Datong City's ancient Yungang Grottoes, are carved out of, and into, the walls themselves. The light of Buddha has been shining here for more than 1,500 years.

Located at the southern foot of Wuzhou Mountain in northwest China, along the once-prominent and ancient Silk Road, Yungang Grottoes is a collection of 51,000 Buddhist rock-cut sandstone statues. They are spread out across 53 separate cave temples and in 252 grottoes, over a 1,000-metre (3,000-ft) surface area in the historic Shanxi province. To the world's 250 million Chinese Buddhists, this landmark is of extra special importance, and a place for them – and all Buddhists – to see effigies of their spiritual leader in a wide variety of shapes and sizes.

Completed over a period of 60 years, during the Northern Wei dynasty, Yungang Grottoes is one of four spiritually significant, and large, grotto complexes throughout China. The others being Mogao Grottoes, Dunhuang; Longmen Grottoes, Luoyang; and Maijishan Grottoes, Tianshui.

Perhaps the most visible and most famous of all the Buddha carvings are the largest ones. There are several 14-metre (46-ft)-tall Buddhas in classic meditation posture, each one an exemplary etching of impossible-seeming rock-carving skill, with intricate and expressive detail visible. The statues – all 59,000 of them – have the added distinction of being considered by art historians to represent the highest level of cave sculpture seen anywhere in the world; multiple visits are required to see a fraction of them.

On the site and surrounding area there are many carvings, in addition to the statues. The caves and alcoves are intricate in design, featuring pillars, altars and shrines.

As a monument to the divine teachings of the Buddha, the grottoes were first set into stone in 465 CE, as decreed by Emperor Xiao Wencheng of the Northern Wei dynasty. It was the Northern Wei people who unified northern China and first established Buddhism as the state religion. It is believed that Tanyao, a renowned monk, advised the emperor to undertake construction of the first cave temples in order to commemorate the five founding emperors of the Northern Wei dynasty – as well as to make the claim, via a statue of himself, that he was a living reincarnation of Buddha. This would serve to secure not only his political survival, but also double up as an insurance that his spiritual legacy would be written in stone forever.

Considering the age of the carvings, the vast majority have survived in excellent condition and it is easy to imagine, when visiting the site, how they would have greeted pilgrims many centuries ago. Owned, preserved and controlled by the Chinese government, the Yungang Grottoes were placed under the protection of the state only in 1961, but daily maintenance and high measures of protection ensure the site will be preserved for many generations to come.

Opposite: When up close and personal with the statues, the level of intricate detail in the carving becomes clear; when viewed from distance the statues are no less impressive.

CHAPTER 6

Living Landmarks

Former places of worship, historical monuments and less traditional sacred sites come in a wide variety of shapes and sizes, and are scattered all over the world. This chapter looks at great monuments, places that have only recently been accepted by organized religions, and an assortment of other fascinating, always exceptional spiritual destinations.

Bodhi Tree

THE SACRED TREE UNDER WHICH THE BUDDHA FOUND NIRVANA

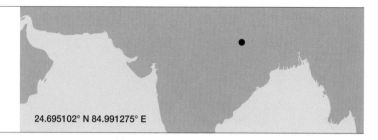

⊛ India

✝ Buddhist

🏛 592 CE

👥 750,000

📅 December–February

🗺 20 km² (7.8 sq. mi.)

24.695102° N 84.991275° E

Under the gaze of the almighty Mahabodhi Temple, and the giant 25-metre (82-ft)-tall Great Buddha statue in India's sacred Bodh Gaya district, grows the holiest Grail in world Buddhism – the Bodhi Tree.

At the foot of this gentle giant of the natural world – a large sacred fig tree (*Ficus religiosa*) – lie the earliest known roots of Buddhism's central teaching: seeking enlightenment. It is here where, in Buddhist texts, it is said that Gautama Buddha, the first and most revered spiritual teacher of Buddhist ideas, first attained the state of nirvana, circa 592 BCE. He was just 29.

Today, for Buddhists the world over, the bodhi tree, or bo tree as it is also known, is believed to possess highly magical forces, including the power to heal and soothe. "It derives its magic from its associations with the life of the Buddha," it is written in the *Srimahabodhi*. "In contagious magic, an object that has any physical link with a being is as powerful as the being himself. The physical link that gives the bodhi tree its power is two-fold: firstly, the fact that the Buddha sat under this tree at the moment of his Enlightenment, and secondly the fact that he spent a whole week, the second week after his Enlightenment, gazing at this tree with motionless eyes."

As has been written for centuries and believed by the half-billion world Buddhists, Gautama Buddha shed his life of material and familial ties, then sat down under this fig tree and began to meditate on the causes of the world's suffering, without eating, drinking, sleeping or moving for seven weeks straight (49 days). His reaching nirvana gifted him with several psychic and physical superpowers including the ability to walk on water and through walls, invisibility, levitation and making copies of himself. On the spot that he sat, a shrine now sits, called Animisalocana cetiya.

The original bodhi tree was first planted around 2,250 years ago. But, that one did not survive long after the Buddha's lifetime. In 254 BCE, according to legend, Tissarakkha, the queen of King Ashoka – an Indian emperor who promoted the advancement of Buddhism across ancient Asia – destroyed the original bodhi tree as she was not in favour of Ashoka's determination to spread Buddhism. The legend continues that Ashoka's daughter, Sanghamitta, broke off a root from the original tree before Tissarakkha destroyed it and took the root somewhere safe, Anuradhapura in Sri Lanka, and planted it. From that root, a new bodhi tree was born and is still alive. In fact, it is understood to be the oldest human-planted tree in the world at 2,300 years old. It was named Sri Maha Bodhiya, in honour of Bodh Gaya.

More than 2,000 visitors visit Bodh Gaya every day, with as many as 60,000 a day during special festivities such as on 8 December, which celebrates the Buddha's enlightenment. Bodhi Day is a religious holiday much revered by Buddhists, and they unite to eat *kheer*, a sweet rice pudding (the Buddha's first meal after his six-year asceticism) and biscuits in the shape of hearts, in celebration of the tree's beautiful leaves.

Opposite (above): The bodhi tree is visible next to the adjacent Mahabodhi Temple; (below) a vast statue of the Buddha stands in the same grounds at Bhod Gaya.

Christ the Redeemer

A COLOSSAL CHRIST ATOP THE SUMMIT OF CORCOVADO MOUNTAIN

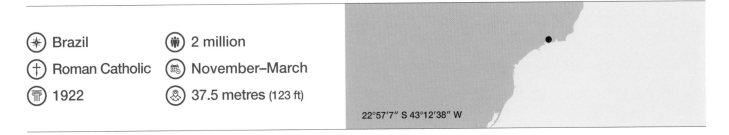

- ✳ Brazil
- ✝ Roman Catholic
- 🏛 1922
- 👥 2 million
- 📅 November–March
- 📍 37.5 metres (123 ft)

22°57'7" S 43°12'38" W

Brazil's Christ the Redeemer, or *Cristo Redentor* in Portuguese, is the world's largest statue of Jesus. But, to the people below, its size is second to its spiritual symbolism. It is a daily reminder of the nation's devotion to Catholicism, and an enduring icon of Jesus as humankind's protector from up on high.

Christ the Redeemer, the enormous statue that overlooks Rio de Janeiro, is simply the most recognizable Christian image in Latin America and unarguably one of the most recognizable religious landmarks in the world. It has been that way for more than a century, since construction began. The Art Deco-style statue was started on 4 April 1922, a day that celebrated the centennial of Brazil's important independence from Portugal.

Built from reinforced concrete and an outer mosaic of more than 6 million triangular soapstone tiles – a natural material found mainly in Brazil – it towers over its host city, piercing the clouds more than half-a-mile up in the sky, sunbathing in enviable sea views of the South Atlantic Ocean.

Despite its position upon the granite peak of Mount Corcovado, which means "hunchback" in Portuguese, this iconic Jesus stands upright on his pedestal at 37.5 metres (123 ft) – two-thirds the height of New York's Statue of Liberty – with his arms horizontally outstretched and spanning 28 metres (92 ft). Once upon a time, intrepid visitors would be required to climb more than 200 steps to reach the plateau at Christ's feet, but today, lifts, escalators and even a train transport millions of pilgrims to the top. Plus you can drive.

Jesus, with his arms open wide, was not the original architectural design. Initially, Heitor da Silva Costa, the statue's central architect, designed Jesus to hold the world in one hand and a cross in the other as he wanted the statue to reclaim Rio's – at the time the capital city of Brazil – Christianity, following a growing swing towards godlessness after the First World War. However, he later changed his mind, agreeing that Christ, with arms open wide, was a much more modern, global, triumphant and welcoming version of the saviour. Today, this iconic version of Christ is much imitated around the world, and is as important to the 65 per cent of the nation's Catholics as any church or place of worship. It is an emblem of both the welcoming spirit of the city of Rio de Janeiro – host of the world-famous Rio Carnival and Copacabana beach, after all – as well as providing spiritual protection for the souls of its 7 million citizens.

The statue is more than just a magnet for 2 million annual pilgrims. It's also a magnet for lightning, getting struck around four times every year. And in 2014, prior to the football World Cup in Rio de Janeiro, lightning struck and broke one of the thumbs on the right hand and damaged the head. Officials worked around the clock to ensure the statue was fixed before kick-off of the first match.

Opposite: At the request of Bishop of Rio, Dom Sebastião Leme, the monument was given a heart on Jesus's chest – but also inside the statue. It is the only part to be decorated inside.

Church of St George

A SUBTERRANEAN CROSS-SHAPED CHURCH, CARVED FROM A SINGLE ROCK

⊛ Ethiopia

✝ Christian

🏛 1200

👥 40,000

📅 19 June (Lalibela feast day)

📍 7 hectares (17 acres)

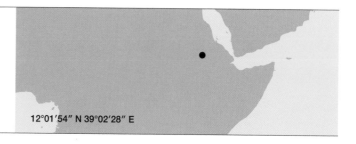

12°01'54" N 39°02'28" E

A millennia ago, Gebre Mesqel Lalibela, the Ethiopian ruler of the Zagwe dynasty (a line of 12th- and 13th-century Ethiopian kings), instructed his people to build a New Jerusalem. The result was 11 of the most distinct rock-hewn churches on earth, the most sacred of which is the Church of St George.

According to Ethiopian legend, upon returning from his 2,574-kilometre (1,600-mile) pilgrimage to the Holy City, in 1187, King Lalibela heard the news that Jerusalem had fallen to Islamic conquest. Muslims now controlled the Holy Land and had put an end to all Christian pilgrimages. Soon after, the king had a dream in which God and his angels appeared before him and instructed him to bring "Heaven down to Earth" and to recreate a new Jerusalem, that all Christian pilgrims could venture to. And so Lalibela did, literally. The king decided that it would be best to carve each church from a single piece of rock, making this heaven out of the earth. He just needed to find a suitable place.

Located 645 kilometres (400 miles) from the nation's capital, Addis Ababa, in a town called Lalibela (named after the king), in the Amhara region, Lalibela commissioned 11 medieval monolithic churches. The last of these rock-hewn churches to be built, the Church of St George, (known locally as Bete Giyorgis), has become the most famous, and is also the most sacred.

The construction of each of the two-storey 12-metre (39-ft)-tall churches involved excavating a giant slab of free-standing tuff – a type of rock made of volcanic ash ejected from a vent during a volcanic eruption – out of the bedrock. Once complete, Lalibela instructed stonemasons to carefully sculpt the stone into a cross shape, to chisel the intricate features on the exterior,

including windows, columns, drainage ditches and catacombs, and, finally, to chisel biblical scenes into the walls of the interior. As a spiritual monument proving Lalibela's devotion to God and Christ, the churches have no equal. However, equally as important, the churches are a testament to the amazing skills of Ethiopia's medieval stonemasons. Perhaps the biggest miracle of all, however, is that each church was carved from top to bottom.

It is unknown if the Church of St George was completed in its creator's lifetime, or if it was constructed after he died to honour his devotion to God, because many details regarding the construction have been lost in the sands of time. Historians believe, however, that the 11 churches took some 24 years to complete (all the way from top to bottom).

Today, these magnificent monuments to Christ have become a popular Christian pilgrimage destination, and they remain a site of huge cultural and religious significance – and mystery – since becoming UNESCO protected in 1978. Frequent earthquakes and atmospheric conditions mean that all 11 churches are in need of much repair and restoration.

Opposite: The Church of St George is made in the form of a cross, and it is connected to several other of the churches by a system of tunnels and trenches.

Hill of Crosses

A SANCTUARY AND SHRINE TO SOLIDARITY AND SACRIFICE

✴ Lithuania

✝ Christian

🏛 1831

👥 120,000

🗓 Last Sunday of July; summer

🗺 6.4 hectares (15.8 acres)

56.0152° N, 23.4153° E

The precise origins and meaning of Lithuania's world-famous Hill of Crosses, or Kryziu Kalnas, remain a mystery waiting to be solved, even to this day. And therein lies its enduring enchantment.

Today, it is believed, almost 200,000 wooden and metal crosses and crucifixes stand proud on top of this small hill, located 12 kilometres (7.5 miles) north of Šiauliai, in northern Lithuania. It is one of the most bewitching and beautiful, spiritually significant sights in the whole of the Baltic region. The number of crosses has more than quadrupled since the early 1990s, following the dissolution of the Soviet Union and when Lithuania gained independence as a country. The hill is also a major pilgrimage site for more than 50,000 Catholics during the summer and spring months. (It is said that only a dozen or so pilgrims venture up the hill during winter, when temperatures plummet to below freezing).

Folklore regarding the Hill of Crosses is recounted in whispers. For some, the first cross was placed on the hill – once occupied by a simple wooden fort – some time in the early 1800s as a reminder of God's heavenly love for the locals below. For others, the hill was the site of an apparition of the Virgin Mary holding the Baby Jesus; it was from this hill that she encouraged believers to adorn it with crosses.

However, it was following the failed rebel uprisings of 1831 and 1863, when neighbours Poland and Lithuania battled against the entrenched tsarist Russian forces (an empire that suppressed religious expression and forbade honouring the dead in cemeteries) that the Hill of Crosses flourished, growing into an iconic shrine to the soldiers who died fighting for its

independence and freedom. Each cross symbolized the defiance of those rebels as well as honouring a religion that was no longer permitted; it was said that the crosses "grew" at night.

For more than a century, Russian administrators repeatedly attempted to destroy the landmark. In April 1961, and a further four more times, thousands of crosses were pulled up and burned. Each time the Hill of Crosses was rebuilt by defiant locals.

The hill is now a sanctuary for tens of thousands of pilgrims who make the journey to place a cross and say a prayer. They now do this not only for those lost fighting for Lithuania, but for Catholics worldwide.

The remote, spiritual site's most popular annual attraction is the Feast of the Hill of Crosses, which occurs annually on the last Sunday of July, and it sees the arrival of a vast throng of pilgrims intent on worship.

On 7 September 1993, Pope John Paul II visited the site and declared it a place for hope, peace, love and sacrifice. "Thank you, Lithuanians", he began, "for this hill of crosses, which testifies to the nations of Europe, and to the whole world, the faith of the people of this land."

Opposite: Cross crafting is a traditional Lithuanian art and an important part of its Roman Catholic culture. The hill is both a shrine for the dead and a celebration of a culture's traditions.

Meteora

SANCTUARIES IN THE SKY, SUSPENDED BETWEEN HEAVEN AND EARTH

⊛ Greece

✝ Greek Orthodox

🏛 1356

👥 2.5 million

📅 March–May

🗺 375 hectares (926 acres)

39°42'5a1" N 21°37'52" E

Placed precipitously, precariously and (perhaps) perilously atop one of Meteora's 1,000 bewitching rock formations – as if delicately placed by the Lord himself – is one of the largest Eastern Orthodox monasteries in the world, second in importance only to Mount Athos.

A UNESCO World Heritage Site since 1988, Meteora remains a location of supreme universal significance. Home to six hanging monasteries that cling to columns of monolithic limestone rocks, "suspended in the air" (in Greek the origin of the word *meteora* comes from the word "meteorite"). These religious sites, all still active places of worship, hover just below heaven and on average 300 metres (984 ft) above sea level, somewhat aptly again, almost precisely in the middle of mainland Greece, near the town of Kalabaka. All are spread out over a beautiful area of 375 hectares (926 acres).

Inaccessible for centuries to all but the most devout and devoted pilgrims and tourists, the seemingly impossible-to-reach monasteries are one of the greatest testaments to humankind's commitment to God. The large, vertical free-standing pillars on which they stand were formed approximately 60 million years ago when earthquakes and erosion separated the limestone from the sand and mud conglomerate. According to local legend, a monk from Mount Athos founded the first Meteora monastery in the 14th century when he was carried to the site by an eagle commanded by God.

After a 45-minute hike to the top of the highest rock, 630 metres (2,066 ft) above sea level, visitors are treated to the Holy Monastery of Great Meteoron, the largest and oldest convent still intact. Between the 14th and 16th centuries, Greek monks built the complex of what was then 20 monasteries on top of the pillars to honour the Virgin Mary. To transport construction materials, and the monks themselves, up the vertical cliff faces, they employed long ladders tied together, and baskets attached to ropes. Today, there are just six monasteries still standing: St Nikolaos Anapafsas, Great Meteoron, Roussanou, Holy Trinity, Varlaam and St Stephen's. Each one is an enduring haven for spiritualists in search of enlightenment above the earth.

The place has not always been respected, however, and history relates that during the Second World War Meteora's monasteries were subject to attacks and looting from enemy troops. Many of the stolen artefacts and paintings were never recovered.

As you would imagine for such picturesque countryside, Meteora has been featured in a number of films, including *For Your Eyes Only*, *Sky Riders* and *Tintin and the Golden Fleece*.

For extra special effect, when it rains the rock formations can change colour, from black to green, due to the moss. And from the top of the Holy Monastery of Great Meteoron, a sunset of epic proportions can be seen as the sun falls beyond the horizon.

Opposite: Theopetra Cave, one of thousands in Meteora, is also known as the place of the oldest man-made structure ever found: a wall. It has been dated back to more than 130,000 years.

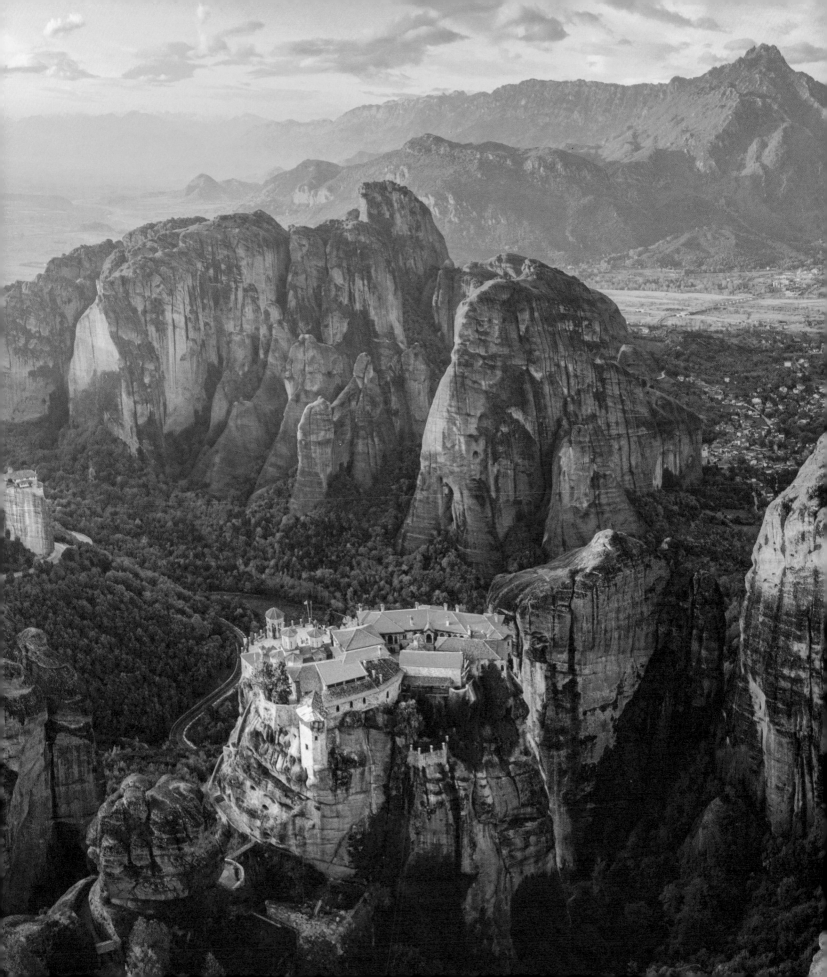

Mont-St-Michel

A SEA-SURROUNDED SANCTUARY OF FAITH THAT POINTS THE WAY TO HEAVEN

- France
- Roman Catholic
- 708 CE
- 3 million
- June–August
- 7 hectares (17 acres)

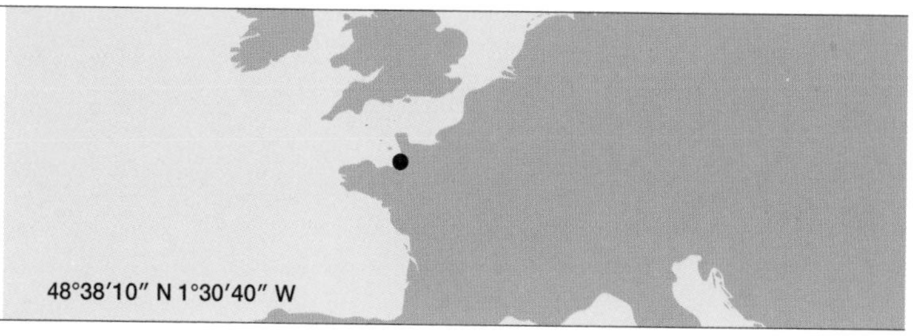
48°38′10″ N 1°30′40″ W

As bewitching as it is beautiful, and as spectacular as it is spiritual, the tidal island of Mont St-Michel is divine in more ways than one.

Monastery. Fortress. Prison. Pilgrimage destination. Sanctuary. Beauty spot. Mont-St-Michel's history unites them all under one glorious, sky-scraping roof. Far from being alone and isolated at high tide, the Mont-St-Michel in Normandy, northwest France, has in fact been acknowledged as a UNESCO World Heritage Site since 1979.

It all began, as many divine things do, with a dream. In 708 CE, Saint Aubert, bishop of nearby Avranches, witnessed an illumination of the Archangel Michael, who defeated Satan in a battle for heaven. The nocturnal vision instructed Saint Aubert to build a chapel on the rocky island not far off the coast, whispering those now-famous words of encouragement, "Build it and they will come".

Build it he did, and come they did, indeed. These days, when not hit by Covid-19 restrictions, the Mont-St-Michel attracts more than three million pilgrims and tourists from all over the world every year to its teeming car parks and busy streets.

And it did not take long for the Mont-St-Michel to become a home away from home, spiritually, even if it took a long time to journey there, physically. To reach the island in the Middle Ages was a revered test of sacrifice, penitence and commitment to God, and a pilgrimage second only to that of Santiago de Compostela in Spain (*see* page 116), as the most important faith quest for Christians. One thousand years ago the island was nicknamed "St Michael in peril of the sea" as it is cut off from land twice a day by a dangerous and powerful high tide. These days a few people get stuck – or worse – every year as the tides turn, the waters rise and all visitors must relocate rapidly.

Its sacred, remote location, in part due to its natural beauty, and the fact that it is a masterpiece of Gothic architecture, has made it all the more enchanting: The iconic Romanesque basilica emerges from the rock, and its spire soars 155 metres (508 ft) into the heavens, a marvel revered as much in the olden days as it is now.

The design of the island is a deliberate testament to the ingenuity of man, as inspired by God. It has multi-tiered structure that represents the hierarchy of the then-feudal society. It is topped by a golden statue of the Archangel Michael, God's representation on earth, followed by the abbey and monastery below it. Underneath those are located the Great Halls, shops and housing, with, finally – right outside the island's walls – are found the fishermen's and farmers' houses.

Mont-St-Michel's counterpart, St Michael's Mount (established 1140), is in Cornwall, southwest England. Although the Cornish version is smaller, it shares the same tidal island characteristics and familiar conical shape. It also shares popularity, with thousands of visitors coming every summer to admire the beauty.

Opposite: Viewed at dawn or dusk, the sun-and-sea combination has a way of lighting up the island in an otherworldly manner. And once the island switches on the spotlights, it can get even more impressive.

Mount Athos

HOLY MOUNTAIN OF GREECE FOR MORE THAN 1,000 YEARS

⊛ Greece

✝ Greek Orthodox

🏛 1054

👥 300,000

📅 15 March–15 June; Sept–Nov

⊗ 335 km² (130 sq. mi.)

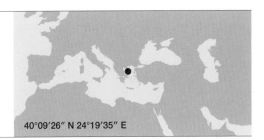

40°09'26" N 24°19'35" E

The steep slopes of Mount Athos have been a safe haven for spirituality, prayer and worship for more than 1,000 years. And they will be for 1,000 more, for sure.

At the top of the mighty peak of Mount Athos, spiking out of the southern tip of the Aegean Sea at an elevation of 2,033 metres (6,670 ft), it is easy to understand why this mass of marble is an enduring legend in Greek mythology and the epicentre for Eastern Orthodoxy. It is the oldest surviving monastic community in the world, and everywhere you look you can see spiritual signs, people and symbols of all shapes and sizes.

In Greek mythology, Athos, one of the Gigantes (a race of giants born of the earth-goddess Gaea, who battled with the Olympians) created Mount Athos when he went to throw it at Poseidon (god of the sea) but it slipped through his fingers and fell to earth. Ever since, the mountain has been the Holy Mountain, Garden of the Mother of God, a sacred place with such deep divinely spiritual roots it is a symbol of paradise on earth.

For 1,000 years, Mount Athos has existed as a monastic republic. It is home to approximately 1,700 monks across 20 monasteries (half of which have survived from the original 40), and spread over 33,000 hectares (81,544 acres) of sprawling chestnut tree forests, nestled at the foot of the mountain, with crashing waves only a few hundred feet below. The oldest monastery on the site is the Megisti Lavra, founded in the 10th century. There, the majority of monks live a simple life, consumed by prayer and chores, practically unchanged since the first of their order arrived 1,000 years before. Many monks choose to live in complete isolation at the mountain's most remote area, Karoulia, where small caves are etched into the

cliff edge. The simplicity of life and lack of distractions from prayer makes them feel closer to God.

The monasteries on Mount Athos are devoted in honour, and praise, of the Virgin Mary, who is said to have visited the mountain and prayed for it to be her own. However, as a result, women (and also children) are forbidden to visit Mount Athos – they are not allowed within 500 metres (1,640 ft) of the shores. This is taken so seriously that even female animals are prohibited. It is believed that the presence of women would distract the monks and tempt them away from their devotion and study.

Mount Athos and its monasteries are not exactly easy to visit for males either, with daily visitors limited in number to 100 lay Orthodox and 10 non-Orthodox males. It is necessary to obtain a special permit for entry, from the Mount Athos Pilgrims Bureau in Thessaloniki. This must be shown before even boarding the ferry that transports people to Mount Athos daily. During the Covid-19 pandemic all visits to the secluded area were curtailed for an entire year.

If you are lucky enough to fulfil the criteria for a visit, a quiet time awaits – a magical, reflective time that will not be forgotten (or possibly repeated) in a hurry.

Opposite: In 1988, Mount Athos became a UNESCO World Heritage Site deemed worthy of outstanding universal value for its rare natural beauty, both flora and fauna, as well as the artistic and spiritual significance of its monasteries.

Mount of Olives

THE ASCENSION OF CHRIST TO HEAVEN HAPPENED HERE

✳ Jerusalem

✝ Christianity, Islam

🏛 0 CE

👥 1 million

📅 April/May

⛰ 808 metres (2,652 ft) (height)

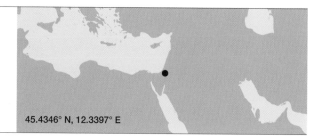

45.4346° N, 12.3397° E

On first glance, the Mount of Olives looks like a long ridge – with a large cemetery and a few other buildings on it – to the east of the Old City of Jerusalem. But when you learn the history of this sacred ground, and see it bathed in golden afternoon sunlight, its millennia-long significance and power both become apparent.

Some places are holy for one single religion. Some places house a number of important sites for multiple faiths. Some places contain a dense concentration of spirituality, almost an embarrassment of religious riches. The Mount of Olives, in East Jerusalem, combines all three – and then some. This must be a contender for the most spiritually concentrated area in the world, with its plethora of tombs, churches, graveyards, shrines and sites of supreme significance.

The Mount of Olives is a fundamental place in the story of Jesus Christ during his time on the earth and is mentioned multiple times in the Bible, notably in the book of Samuel as the place of Jesus's ascent and then in the book of Zechariah during the prophecy of the end of days. It is written that Jesus visited the site multiple times as a teacher, but even more significantly on the night before his betrayal. The famous Garden of Gethsemane, located on the western slope of the hill, was where Jesus and his disciples sang together shortly before his betrayal. According to the scriptures, it was from the Mount of Olives that Jesus ascended into heaven, so the entire hill is steeped in Christian lore from top to bottom.

As you would have guessed from the name, the Mount of Olives was once a large olive grove, although there have been structures on the site for many thousands of years. The huge

Jewish cemetery alone has been active for more than 3,000 years, making it the oldest continuously used cemetery in the world. It contains an estimated 150,000 graves. In Judæo-Christian beliefs, it is on the Mount of Olives that Jesus will appear in his second coming. It is for this additional reason that burial in the cemetery is of the upmost importance for people of the Jewish faith.

The peak usually regarded as the top of the Mount of Olives is at 808 metres (2,652 ft) above sea level and houses the Augusta Victoria Hospital. Other structures near the top include a joint mosque and Christian chapel, which was built on the site at which Jesus is reputed to have ascended into heaven.

For those lucky enough to walk around this vast spiritual site (it is easily accessible from the centre of Jerusalem), the spiritual nature of the area is apparent with every step. And despite now looking more like an everyday hillside, clues to the ancient past still exist, in the shape of ancient olive trees, some of which would have stood at the time of Christ.

Opposite: The Mount of Olives is home to places of worship of multiple faiths. On the top of the ridge can be found a Lutheran church, a mosque, a Russian Orthodox church, a Catholic church and a Jewish cemetery. On the other side of the valley stands the Dome of the Rock.

Padmanabhaswamy Temple

GOLD, MYSTERIOUS VAULTS AND DIVINE WORSHIP COMBINE IN INDIA'S RICHEST SHRINE

- (✵) India
- (†) Hindu
- (🏛) 1858
- (👥) 5 million
- (📅) October/November; March/April
- (📍) 51 hectares (126 acres)

8°28'58" N 76°56'37" E

This fascinating, beautiful, shining temple is dedicated to Lord Vishnu and is situated close to the Padmatheertha Pond, which – when the light is right – fully reflects the temple's gleaming roof in the waters below. But much is whispered about the temple and the vast, valuable treasures that are contained in the vaults below...

Sometimes a place of worship is featured in the news. Maybe a record number of visitors. Perhaps the discovery of a rare artefact once considered lost. Maybe even the vision of a deity brings an inevitable 15 minutes of fame. But Padmanabhaswamy Temple, in the big, bustling city of Kerala, is rarely out of the news, mostly due to the speculation of the hugely valuable contents of its numerous vaults, in particular the mysterious vault B.

But taking a step back, and looking at the placement and design of this wonderful place of worship, there has been a temple on this site since the 6th century, when a structure was recorded in medieval Tamil literature. It was not until the 16th century, however, that the ornate *gopuram* (ornate roofing structure) was installed. In 1566, the seven-tier *gopuram* was built and afterwards covered in gold. And gold is part of what contributes to the controversy – and mystery – that the temple is most famous for.

As with all Hindu temples, only members of that faith are permitted entry, making this an unlikely tourist destination. This is a shame for those wishing to visit, for the temple's construction and design style are very distinct, with many corridors, doorways, shrines and, of course, vaults that will never be viewed by anyone non-Hindu. That does not mean this temple is not worth a visit, of course. The ornate roofing, stone-carved statues and beautiful door are unlike any you will encounter elsewhere and will remain long in your memory.

As for the vaults, much has been written, reported and speculated about them over the years. What is without a doubt is that the temple is fabulously wealthy, with estimates putting its assets at more than an almost-unbelievable value of US$1 trillion. Most of this is stored in the many underground vaults, numbered between A and H, and where are stored a vast number of hugely valuable coins, idols, statues, ceremonial costumes and all sorts of other pieces with enormous worth.

But it is not wealth that makes this a fascinating spiritual centre; this temple would be just as stunning if the vaults were empty. It is the centuries of belief, worship and prayer that contribute to its stature as a deeply faithful place.

Opposite (above): The temple is usually lit up at night, giving beautiful reflections in the nearby Padmatheertha Pond.
Opposite (below): A close-up of the temple's intricate *goparum* carvings on the roof.

Père Lachaise Cemetery

A VAST TOWN OF THE DEAD WITHIN THE CITY OF LIGHTS

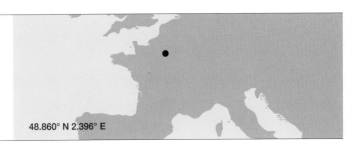

⊛ France

✝ Multifaith

🏛 1804

👥 3.5 million

📅 All year round

🗺 45 hectares (111 acres)

48.860° N 2.396° E

Walking through the winding streets and alleyways of Père Lachaise Cemetery is like taking a journey back in time to another world: a world of the dead, where the spirits of the deceased live on in their ornate tombs scattered around the most visited necropolis in the world.

Like many innovations, buildings and administrative structures in France, the Cimetière Père Lachaise has its foundations in the time of Napoléon Bonaparte; for it was the emperor who established the space as a cemetery in the east of Paris. The architect he used was Alexandre-Theodore Brongniart, who claimed that English-style gardens were his inspiration, and the uneven paths, hills and seemingly random natural and man-made elements attest to this. The cemetery was popular right from the first year it opened, in 1804. It is now estimated that one million souls reside within the high walls of the cemetery, which has been expanded numerous times, so busy has it proved.

Père Lachaise is steeped in history, and it counts some of the world's most famous writers, artists, performers and politicians among its residents. Edith Piaf, Yves Montand, Molière, Jean de la Fontaine, Modigliani, Pissarro, Delacroix, Apollinaire, Chopin, Proust and Balzac are just a few of the names. And as for the non-French, the most famous resident is for some strange reason Jim Morrison, who occupies a much-visited plot that is covered with flowers, trinkets and graffiti. And there are plenty more notable non-natives, including Oscar Wilde, Max Ophuls, Isadora Duncan, Maria Callas and many others.

And it is not just the stature of the people who are buried here that make this such a fascinating, unique place. The cemetery would be a deeply engrossing place to spend a day (many days),

visiting the tombs of such significant ancestors if it were laid out in careful, clean rows, but it is the style of the memorials that adds another level of interest. From tiny headstones and small memorials to giant mausoleums and massive monuments, everything is placed seemingly randomly around the cemetery. And what a random mixture it is, too: a winding cobbled street leads to a line of graves on a hill. A large pagoda looks down on some crumbling, overlapping tombstones. There is a monument to holocaust survivors, there are chapels, houses and simple graves. There are ornate statues, simple plain stones, pianos, carved flowers, swords and all sorts of other objects preserved in stone. It is the combination of all of this that brings visitors in record numbers to the cemetery. More than one million people visit every year to walk through the streets, armed with a map that shows the all-important locations.

People of all faiths are buried here – an important notion for the land of *fraternité, égalité et liberté* – and people of all faiths are free to visit. And a walk around Père Lachaise, whatever the weather, brings us spiritually closer to the past.

Opposite: Seen from above, the cemetery looks small and manageable, but when you enter through one of the many huge gates, it becomes quickly apparent that you are walking through a vast, sprawling necropolis.

Quito

AN ENTIRE CITY RICH IN HISTORY, CULTURE, RELIGION AND SPIRITUALITY

⊛ Ecuador

✝ Multifaith

🏛 708 CE

👤 3 million

📅 June–August

📍 2,850 m (9,350 ft) (altitude)

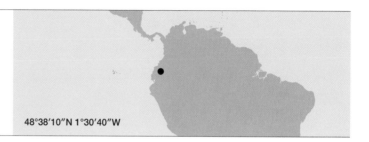

48°38'10"N 1°30'40"W

The oldest capital city in South America, Quito has been an occupied settlement for thousands of years. High up in the mountains, nestled between ridges, it has been subject to a wide variety of influences throughout its lifetime, surviving multiple occupations, invasions and earthquakes.

Quito is a city in the heavens, physically to start with, but also spiritually, as we'll see. And the close-to-God symbolism doesn't end there. The modern city we know today was founded by the Spanish in the 16th century, but the modern city was constructed on the foundations of an ancient Inca settlement. Many of the streets and plazas were carried over from the original city, as the Spanish invaders were mindful of the intelligent city design of the ancestors of the countries they invaded.

Known as San Francisco de Quito when it was founded, it is hard to think of this modern, sprawling city as a peaceful haven where human and nature seemed to peacefully co-exist, but that is very much how Quito was seen for centuries, even well into the colonial period of its history.

But when it comes to the spiritual nature of a city, many wonder how can a bustling metropolis be rich in spiritual nature? The answer is in the multitude of spiritual centres that the city possesses, combined with its amazing location and also includes its rich, mysterious Inca – and older – history. The oldest known remains that have been located to date are some fragments of glass that are reputed to date all the way back to 8000 BCE. After this, the Quitu people lived in the area, known as Quito for the first time around 500 CE. And written records show these people were displaced by 1000 CE by people from further afield. And then, by the 15th century, the Incas had established their city on

the slopes. Sadly, very little of the city from this era has been preserved, and Quito's UNESCO status as a World Heritage Centre is based more around the extremely well protected old city, which is the best preserved in South America.

On the contemporary, spiritual front there are many churches, cathedrals and a basilica. And surveying the city, from the hill known as El Panecillo, is a monument to the Virgin Mary. This 41-metre (135-ft)-tall statue was commissioned in 1976 but is based on an original sculpture from 1732. It is visible from almost everywhere in Quito.

On the less contemporary front, and away from organized religion, Quito is famous for its *curanderas* – traditional healers who source their herbs from the forests and plains from miles around in the nature-rich Andes. They can heal many things with their millennia-old natural remedies, and some even famously claim to have a cure for bad luck; it is yet another question of belief.

All who visit Quito, for whatever reason, will attest that something special exists here, from the streets to the hills and from the churches to the yogic retreats.

Opposite: (above): Downtown Quito – the Basilica del Voto Nacional. **Opposite (below):** The Panecillo statue of the Virgin Mary.

Taj Mahal

A CROWN PALACE BUILT IN PERFECT SYMMETRY FOR THE ETERNAL LOVE OF A PRINCESS

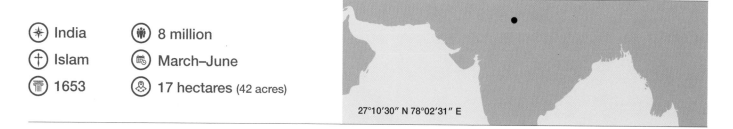

- ✳ India
- ✝ Islam
- 🏛 1653
- 👥 8 million
- 🗓 March–June
- ⛲ 17 hectares (42 acres)

27°10'30" N 78°02'31" E

In the city of Agra, located on the right bank of the famous Yamuna river, the second-largest tributary of India's most sacred Ganges river, the Taj Mahal is perhaps the world's most beautiful, and iconic, monument to love … after life. But its beauty is more than just skin deep.

Covering the same size surface area as 20 football pitches, the Taj Mahal is as sizeable as it is perfectly symmetrical, a feat of incredible architectural engineering. Commissioned in 1632 by the fifth Mughal emperor Shah Jahan (who ruled from 1628 to 1658) as a tomb for his late wife, a Persian princess and Agra native, Mumtaz Mahal. She had died the previous year giving birth to the couple's 13th child. Her tomb is at the heart of this sprawling complex, which also includes a mosque and extensive gardens. Buried next to her is Shah Jahan himself.

Grief-stricken after the death of his beloved, the Emperor ordered 20,000 labourers to start work on a project that would take more than two decades to complete. The plan was to build that Taj Mahal – Persian for "crown palace" – as an enduring symbol of his adoration and affection for his wife… as well as, of course, a testament of his wealthy empire's legacy of artistic and scientific accomplishment.

Made of red sandstone and covered in glowing white marble, today the Taj Mahal is considered an extra special sacred symbol because of the hypnotizing ability of its building blocks to change colour. They can be anything from bright pink at sunrise to bright white at noon, and blue in the illumination of the moon. The changing colour of this magical mausoleum is said to be linked, at least poetically if not set in stone, to the stages of love and pain that the emperor experienced following his courtship, wedding and subsequent married life to Mumtaz, his favourite wife. For the more than eight million visitors who make the pilgrimage here every year, seeing the Taj Mahal all lit up is akin to waking up in a dream-like place of great beauty and calmness, such as Jannah, the garden of paradise in Islamic scripture. For those who are lucky enough to witness the Taj Mahal up close and personal will be bonded once and for all to it in its deep, spiritual power and will never forget the experience.

Viewing the palace head-on from its world-famous photograph spot (see opposite), the Taj Mahal's shape is in the form of a solitary tear suspended on the horizon; a symbol of the shah's eternal sorrow. The largest teardrop is, in fact, the largest of the palace's domes. It is affectionately known as the Onion Dome, and it rises to about 35 metres (115 feet) high, and beneath which Mumtaz and her king – and her love – are buried.

The Taj Mahal was designated as a UNESCO World Heritage Site in 1983 as "the jewel of Muslim art in India and one of the universally admired masterpieces of the world's heritage". It is, unsurprisingly, one of the most visited sites in the world.

Opposite: Outside, the beautiful white marble reflects in the calm waters in front. Inside, the walls of the Taj Mahal are engraved with verses from the Quran about the journey to paradise.

Varanasi

PILGRIMAGE, DEATH AND MOURNING ON THE BANK OF THE GANGES

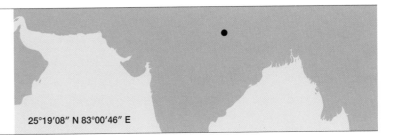

- ✳ India
- ✝ Hindu
- 🏛 1800 BCE
- 👥 2.5 million
- 📅 All year round
- 📍 82 km² (32 sq. mi)

25°19'08" N 83°00'46" E

India's cultural capital is a vast, teeming city on the edge of the Ganges river. It holds special spiritual significance for the entire nation, particularly the Hindus, who come to the many sacred ghat cremation grounds to send the dead on their way to the afterlife. It's a busy place...

Varanasi is known as the spiritual heart of India, and it is said to be the oldest continuously populated city in the world. Evidence has been uncovered that shows the area around was home to people as far back as 1800 BCE. But the city has been famed for a wide variety of reasons, not least as the home of Buddhism, for it was close by in Sarnath that the Buddha visited and gave his first sermon, called "The Setting in Motion the Wheels of Dharma". There is now a monument on that spot, in the park where the speech was delivered.

Fundamental to the Hindu religion is the river Ganges – India's "mother river" – which flows through Varanasi and is a centre of myth, spiritual significance and ritual. As Jawaharlal Nehru said, "The Ganga is the river of India, beloved of her people, round which are intertwined her racial memories, her hopes and fears..." Indians believe the entire 2,525-kilometre (1,569-mile) length of the river to be sacred, and many rituals are associated with the waters. In Varanasi, on the banks of the Ganges are a number of ghats, 88 in total. These river-front places are of deep spiritual significance and feature steps that lead down to the lapping waters below. Ghats have different purposes, some are for bathing, others cremations and other rituals. In the most famous, Manikarnika Ghat, bodies of the dead are cremated, for in Hindu religion this is the best way for a body to be sent to the afterlife, and Varanasi is the best place for this to happen.

In what is a further level of complexity in Indian society, the dead bodies are only handled by Dom people. They are outcasts from the community, but who form an essential part of the ritual cycle of birth, death and afterlife.

Dashashwamedh Ghat is another of the most prominent ghats, standing not far from the golden dome and roofing of the famous Vishwanath Temple in Varanasi. It is certainly the most colourful and the first nightly ritual is performed by priests at 7 p.m. every night of every day of the year. But Varanasi's spiritual significance is not just about its proximity to the river Ganges, it is also tied to the heart of this city, a centre of music, shopping and learning, as well as of worship and ancient history.

In Hindu mythology, Varanasi was founded by Shiva, following a fight with other deities. Shiva later dropped the severed head of one of them, Brahma, understood that the site where it fell was very holy, and decided it would be the ideal site for a new city. The city was called Kashi in ancient times, becoming Banaras later, and was not known as Varanasi until 1948.

Opposite: There are many ghats (sacred river fronts) in Varanasi, the most famous being Manikarnika Ghat, which welcomes many elderly people who are preparing themselves for one final journey.

Wat Rong Khun

AN ARTISTICALLY DESIGNED MODERN CENTRE OF WORSHIP AND ENLIGHTENMENT

✳ Thailand

✝ Buddhist

🏛 1997

👥 2 million

📅 Nov–Dec ("Light Fest")

📍 2.6 hectares (6.4 acres)

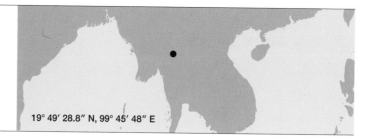

19° 49' 28.8" N, 99° 45' 48" E

A temple. An art installation. A sculpture. The privately owned Buddhist place of spiritual education and worship at Wat Rong Khun is a truly unique place, the vision of a local artist who thought his unique dream would bring millions of people flocking to his ornate palace of education. He was right.

Most Buddhist temples around the world are colourful. Most Buddhist temples (in Thailand at least), feature a red and gold colour scheme. Most places of worship don't have images from *Star Wars* and *Spider-Man*. But Wat Rong Khun is not like most places, full stop. Wat Rong Khun, situated in the very north of Thailand, is nearly 800 kilometres (500 miles) from the country's capital, Bangkok, in the south. It is close to Chiang Rai, a small town, and is home to an artist with a huge vision.

Chalermchai Kositpipat is a local visual artist and painter. He saw that the temple at Wat Rong Khun was in a state of disrepair and decided to raise the funds himself to have it restored. But not content with simply patching it up, he went for a complete rebuild in a totally modern design that fuses traditional aspects of temple structure with modern architecture, as well as mixing traditional Buddhist deities and symbolic creatures with contemporary super heroes, robots and other characters from fiction. "Why?" is a not unreasonable question to ask of Kositpipat. He said that he designed and built the temple as an offering to the Buddha and that, as a devout Buddhist, he hopes by his actions to attain immortal life: "Death can stop my dream, but cannot stop my project."

The temple and the grounds are not finished, and, similar to Barcelona's Sagrada Família (*see* page 88) – another spiritual venue where the lines between art, worship and spirituality overlap – there is no realistic date for completion. But even in this ostensibly unfinished state, the complex and associated buildings and landmarks have a number of fantastic features, and the attention to detail is wondrous. In order to gain entry to the main temple (the *ubosot*), visitors must cross the Bridge of the Cycle of Rebirth, where hundreds of hands sprout from the earth and reach skywards. This symbolizes humankind's freedom from its suffering, one of Buddhism's central tenets. Guarding the long entrance to the *ubosot* are two large statues representing the judges of the fate of humankind. In the *ubosot* the walls are painted with a number of contemporary figures – even Neo from the film *The Matrix* makes an appearance.

From November to December 2019, there was a "Light Fest" in the temple, which involved a huge, colourful illumination of many of the buildings in the complex. Photographs and videos of the event affirm that this is a truly unique place to visit, and the idea of spiritual entertainment is as original as the rest of the inspiration behind the setting. Whatever time of year you visit, this unique place is sure to make you reflect deeply.

Opposite: The temple at Wat Rong Khun is a stunning visual feast for the eyes. Although much of it is white, there is a golden temple, a mirrored section and an unbelievable amount of intricate detailing.

INDEX

PICTURE CREDITS